WHEN TIMES ARE TOUGH

5 Scriptures That Will Help You Get through Almost Anything

JOHN BYTHEWAY

DESERET BOOK

SALT LAKE CITY, UTAH

Library of Congress Cataloging-in-Publication Data

Bytheway, John, 1962-
  When times are tough : 5 Scriptures that will help you get through almost anything / John Bytheway.
    p. cm.
  ISBN 1-59038-358-3 (hardbound : alk. paper)
  1. Christian life—Mormon authors. 2. Book of Mormon—Criticism, interpretation, etc. 3. Bible—Criticism, interpretation, etc. I. Title.
  BX8656.B894 2004
  248.4'89332—dc22

                        2004014437

Printed in the United States of America   70582
Phoenix Color Corporation, Hagerstown, MD

10 9 8 7 6 5 4 3 2 1

ETHEL NOALL JARMAN, 1903–2004

To my grandma, the "Ethelgizer," who just kept going and going and going. Grandma endured many tough times during her long life but remained cheerful, hopeful, and curious to the end. (She bought and learned to use a computer at age eighty-five.) Gracious, loving, and delightful, Grandma truly had sunshine in her soul, and her warmth and faith radiated to everyone around her. We miss you, Grandma!

TABLE OF CONTENTS

ACKNOWLEDGMENTS

I wish to thank the many wonderful people at Deseret Book for helping me put this book together, including Chris Schoebinger for encouraging and shaping the project, Michael Morris for his editing skills, Shauna Gibby for her artistic talents, and Tonya Facemyer for her typesetting. Thanks also to Cory Maxwell and Sheri Dew for their friendship and support. Finally, I'm grateful to my wife, Kimberly, and my children—Ashley, Andrew, Natalie, and Matthew—who make every day an adventure.

I can't think of any more powerful weapons than faith and a knowledge of the scriptures in the which are contained the Word of God. One so armoured and one so prepared with those weapons is prepared to go out against the enemy [and] is more to be feared than the enemies of light.

—HAROLD B. LEE,
BYU Speeches of the Year,
November 9, 1954

WHAT ARE WE LEANING ON?

A few years ago, a former wrestler-turned-politician referred to organized religion as a crutch for weak-minded people who need strength in numbers. Nothing new there. Similar comments have been made thousands of times and for thousands of years. In the Book of Mormon, Korihor characterized believers as "bound down under a foolish and vain hope," which belief was "the effect of a frenzied mind" (Alma 30:13–16.)

As one who has had to rely on the Lord's strength from time to time, I don't mind being referred to as weak-minded, and I admit I often find strength in numbers. The fact is, I *am* weak, and I frequently lean on my religion and my fellowship with the Saints to see me through difficult times. But calling religion a crutch is a gross minimization.

Yes, the gospel gives us something to lean on, to be sure, but our religion is much, much more.

About the time I began working on this book, my father passed away after suffering for many years with Parkinson's disease. He had joined the Church at age twenty-four, married, and served a full-time mission—in that order. We were proud of all he had accomplished and of the legacy of faith and testimony he left his posterity.

Surrounding his bed at the time of his passing were his wife of fifty-three years, his six children, and a few of his numerous grandchildren. I will never forget the many feelings that rushed through our hearts at the moment he left us. We had been unable to communicate with him for the previous three days, and when he finally released his last breath, all of us experienced a strange mixture of sorrow and celebration. In fact, one of my sisters, expecting Dad's spirit to be somewhere in the room, looked upward and tearfully exclaimed, "Good job, Dad!"

The feelings of sorrow mixed with celebration remained throughout the viewing and funeral. As I watched my family go through that difficult time, I didn't see what the former pro-wrestler described. I didn't see a group of weaklings leaning on crutches. I saw something entirely different. I witnessed the power, the *real, sustaining power*, that came from our testimonies of the gospel. It supported us, filled us with hope and expectation, and even allowed us to smile and laugh in the midst of our loss.

My father's passing brought me further confirmation of something I had always known. Yes, we are weak, and we do need something to lean on at times. But if you look close, you'll find that what we are leaning on is not a crutch but a sword.

LESSONS FROM LITTLETON

A few days after the terrible events at Columbine High School in 1999, Brother Rob Hildebrandt called me to ask if I could come talk to the LDS youth who attended the Columbine seminary. This was the most intimidating speaking invitation I had ever received. I was honored to be invited, but I spent a few sleepless nights trying to think of what I could possibly say to the young people, some of whom had witnessed the shooting and one of whom had been severely wounded.

I knew they needed more than just fun stories about growing up, attending high school, and going on dates. They needed more than just *Chicken Soup for the Teenage Soul,* as helpful as such books can be. They didn't need a crutch; they needed power. They were hungry for answers, and they wanted them from a source they knew they could trust.

I eventually put together a presentation I titled "Five

Scriptures That Will Help You Get through Almost Anything." As I delivered my talk, I was thrilled to see the young people eagerly looking up the scriptures I cited. In response to an event that shook many of them to the core, these young people paused to lean on their swords. They found power, perspective, hope, and answers in the word of God, and they felt the spirit of the Lord that always accompanies a sincere study of the scriptures.

On that occasion, I was reminded that the Apostle Paul described many pieces of equipment that make up the armor of God, such as the "breastplate of righteousness," the "shield of faith," and the "helmet of salvation." The final item Paul mentioned—the only offensive weapon in a list of defensive armor—was the "sword of the Spirit, which is the word of God" (Ephesians 6:14–17). I believe that Paul deliberately described the sword as a symbol of two different things—the *Spirit* and the *scriptures*. The fact is that the Spirit of the Lord is in the scriptures, and reading the scriptures allows the Spirit to confirm their truthfulness.

Yes, Latter-day Saints often lean on their religion for support during difficult times. But when difficulties pass, as they always do, our religion enables us to "rise in might with the sword of truth and right,"[1] ready to strike a blow for goodness and virtue.

Fortunately, when we need wisdom to help us govern

our lives, we have better sources than retirees of the Worldwide Wrestling Federation, the hollow teaching of Hollywood, or the shifting psychology of pop culture. We have so much more. Within the covers of our standard works is a modern-day "school of the prophets," where class is constantly in session and the tuition is free. On the faculty is a team of spiritual giants, many of whom have conversed personally with the Lord. All we have to do is open and read in order to be tutored by Moses, Isaiah, Nephi, Alma, Paul, and many others.

Each of us can expect to experience things in our lives that may also shake us to the core, but we know where to find the answers that will help us survive and thrive. We know that we can look to the word of God—our sword to fight our battles with the world and something to lean on when times are tough.

SOME "ANSWERS" HAVE A LOW SHELF LIFE

Many years ago, Dr. Albert Einstein was teaching graduate-level physics at Princeton University. After administering an exam to his students, Dr. Einstein and his graduate assistant were walking across campus. The assistant was carrying the completed tests and suddenly asked, "Dr. Einstein, isn't this the same test you gave last year?" "Yes," replied the scientist. The assistant was incredulous. "Dr. Einstein, how could you give the same test two years in a row?" he asked. Dr. Einstein replied matter-of-factly, "Since last year, the answers have changed."[2]

Most college students have paid dearly for a college textbook, only to have the bookstore refuse to take it back at the end of the semester. It happened to me with a biology text. "I'm sorry," the bookstore employee said, "we're not using that text next semester. I realize you paid $75 for it, but we can only give you $5." What happened? The answers changed.

I naively saved many of my college textbooks, thinking they might be useful to me later in life. Unfortunately, they are all obsolete. After only a few years, the answers have changed. Now my old texts are nothing but fodder destined for Deseret Industries. The scriptures, on the other hand, contain answers that do not change. Some books in the scriptures are thousands of years old, but they are still true.

ABOUT THIS BOOK

This book is divided into five chapters. Chapter one is an expanded version of the remarks I prepared for the youth of the Columbine High School seminary. Chapters two through five illustrate that the gospel is not only something to lean on through difficult times but also a blessing that can help us in every aspect of daily living.

These chapters include scriptures that will bless our marriage and family life, fill us with faith, and motivate us to action.

The breadth and depth of the standard works make it difficult to select only five scriptures on any topic. You will be able to find dozens, perhaps hundreds, of other scriptures that have strengthened you and helped you. What I have done here is simply chosen a few scriptures that have blessed my life, hoping that they may bless the lives of others as well.

NOTES

1. "Hope of Israel," *Hymns of The Church of Jesus Christ of Latter-day Saints* (Salt Lake City: The Church of Jesus Christ of Latter-day Saints, 1985), no. 259.

2. As cited in Brian Tracy, *Thinking Big* (New York: Simon and Schuster Audio, 1997), audiocassette, tape 1, side B.

CHAPTER ONE

FIVE SCRIPTURES THAT WILL HELP YOU GET THROUGH ALMOST ANYTHING

❧ I once read of an old Chinese saying that states, "May you live in interesting times." Our times are a little too interesting for most of us, and I suspect we would prefer a little less chaos. In the middle of this mess, we sometimes hear the younger generation say, "I'm bored." If the youth of the Church are bored, we can assure them that the last days are going to get more intense and more "interesting" very soon. The faithful will be anything but bored.

The past few years have produced an acceleration of tragic headlines. We've seen it all—from natural disasters to international terrorism to the breakdown of families. Innocent people, even children, are not spared. Why do bad things happen? Philosophers and theologians have

1

wrestled with that problem for centuries, and I won't pretend to be smarter than they are.

However, as Latter-day Saints, we have something most philosophers and theologians don't have. We have revelation, both ancient and modern. We have additional ancient scripture, such as the Book of Mormon and the Pearl of Great Price, and we have modern scripture, such as the Doctrine and Covenants. We also have revelation from modern prophets.

And while we may never know *all* of the answers in this life, there are some things we know to be true that come from a place where answers don't change. Thus, we can approach the events of the last days with a different question: What *do* we know? What do we know *for sure*, without a doubt, that can help us survive in these interesting times?

SCRIPTURE ONE:
"[We] know that [God] loveth his children" (1 Nephi 11:17)

Early in the Book of Mormon, an angel asked Nephi a tough question: "Knowest thou the condescension of God?" Nephi answered with something he knew and something he didn't know: "I know that he loveth his children; nevertheless, I do not know the meaning of all things" (1 Nephi 11:16–17). Nephi's answer is a perfect statement for us to remember in times of trial. We don't know the meaning of all things. We don't have all of the answers to explain all of the tragedies in the world and in our neighborhood. However, we do *know* and we are *sure* that God loves his children.

If our testimonies are strong on this point and if we feel the absolute assurance that God loves us, we will change our questions. We won't ask, "Why did this happen?" or "Why doesn't God care about me?" Instead, our questions will become, "What can I learn from this experience?" or "How does the Lord want me to handle this?" Elder Richard G. Scott taught:

> When you face adversity, you can be led to ask many questions. Some serve a useful purpose; others do not. To ask, Why does this have to happen to me? Why do I have to suffer this, now? What have I done to cause this? will lead you into blind alleys. It really does no good to ask questions that reflect opposition to the will of God. Rather ask, What am I to do? What am I to learn from this experience? What am I to change? Whom am I to help? How can I remember my many blessings in times of trial? Willing sacrifice of deeply held personal desires in favor of the will of God is very hard to do. Yet, when you pray with real

conviction, "Please let me know Thy will" and "May Thy will be done," you are in the strongest position to receive the maximum help from your loving Father.[1]

One of the mistakes we often make is to believe that all trials come because we did something wrong. A friend of mine described two types of adversity experienced by the Lord's people throughout the scriptures. He called them "penalty adversity," or adversity that comes as a result of disobedience (such as the wanderings of the children of Israel), and "growth adversity," or adversity that is simply part of our second estate but from which we can grow and progress if we choose. Yes, some trials come because of our own disobedience, but many trials are simply part of living in this fallen world.

The scriptures contain many examples of righteous people who have suffered: Abraham, Abinadi, Joseph of Egypt, Paul, Joseph Smith, and even Jesus Christ. Brother Truman Madsen once asked President Hugh B. Brown why the Lord would put Abraham through the horrible experience of thinking that he had to sacrifice his own son. Abraham had been promised numerous seed that would bless all of the families of the world, yet he was asked to sacrifice his only son! Obviously God knew Abraham's heart. God knew that Abraham would be willing to do anything he was commanded. So why did the Lord put Abraham through such a test? President Brown answered, "Abraham needed to learn something about Abraham."[2] President George Q. Cannon agreed:

> Now, why did the Lord ask such things of Abraham? Because, knowing what his future would be and that he would be the father of an innumerable posterity, he was determined to test him. God did not do this for His own sake; for He knew by His foreknowledge what Abraham would do; but the purpose was to impress upon Abraham a lesson, and to enable him to attain unto knowledge that he could not obtain in any other way. That is why God tries all of us. It is not for His own knowledge; for He knows all things beforehand. He knows all your lives and everything you will do. But He tries us for our own good, that we may know ourselves; for it is most important that a man should know himself. He required Abraham to submit to this trial because He intended to give him glory, exaltation and honor; He intended to make him a king and a priest, to share with Himself the glory, power and dominion which He exercised.[3]

All of us experience growth adversity from time to time, and it helps us to learn something about ourselves. God already knows what we're made of, but perhaps he wants us to learn what we're made of. Personally, I have learned much more from my tough times than from my easy times. When I look back on some of my trials, I can see how they have blessed me. As someone once said, "A blessing is anything that moves us closer to God." In that way, I can see that many of my trials have blessed my life. I have found great comfort in this statement by Orson F. Whitney:

> No pain that we suffer, no trial that we experience is wasted. It ministers to our education, to the development of such qualities as patience, faith, fortitude and humility. All that we suffer and all that we endure, especially when we endure it patiently, builds up our characters, purifies our hearts, expands our souls, and makes us more tender and charitable, more worthy to be called the children of God . . . and it is through sorrow and suffering, toil and tribulation, that we gain the education that we come here to acquire and which will make us more like our Father and Mother in heaven.[4]

What a list! A trial "ministers to our education," develops our "patience, faith, fortitude and humility," "builds our characters, purifies our hearts, expands our souls," and "makes us more tender and charitable." While our trials are bitter at the time we experience them, who would want to miss out on all that growth—growth that might not be possible any other way? Elder Neal A. Maxwell observed:

> How can you and I really expect to glide naively through life, as if to say, "Lord, give me experience, but not grief, not sorrow, not pain, not opposition, not betrayal, and certainly not to be forsaken. Keep from me, Lord, all those experiences which made Thee what Thou art! Then, let me come and dwell with Thee and fully share Thy joy!"[5]

When we properly view our trials, we can see that a loving Father in Heaven sometimes allows us to experience growth adversity for our own good. And when we grow through our own adversity, we may become a tool in the Lord's hands to help others through their problems. Who better to help someone who is experiencing a difficult trial than one who has experienced it himself? The trials we endure enable us to help others endure their trials.

The scriptures attest that we're going to have trials. Welcome to earth. But we know God loves his children. Nowhere is this thought expressed more beautifully than in this verse from Romans: "For I am persuaded, that neither death, nor life, nor angels, nor principalities, nor powers, nor things present, nor things to come, nor height, nor depth, nor any other creature, shall be able to separate us from the love of God, which is in Christ Jesus our Lord" (Romans 8:38–39).

Sometimes bad things happen to good people. We don't know the meaning of all things, but we know God loves his children! And because he loves us, he will never desert us. President Cannon taught:

> No matter how serious the trial, how deep the distress, how great the affliction, [God] will never desert us. He never has, and He never will. He cannot do it. It is not His character. He is an unchangeable being; the same yesterday, the same today, and He will be the same throughout the eternal ages to come. We have found that God. We have made Him our friend, by obeying His Gospel; and He will stand by us. We may pass through the fiery furnace; we may pass through deep waters; but we shall not be consumed nor overwhelmed. We

shall emerge from all these trials and difficulties
the better and purer for them, if we only trust
in our God and keep His commandments.[6]

How much does God love us? The scriptures answer:
"For God so loved the world, that he gave his only be-
gotten Son, that whosoever believeth in him should not
perish, but have everlasting life" (John 3:16) and "Greater
love hath no man than this, that a man lay down his life
for his friends" (John 15:13).

SCRIPTURE TWO:
We know that God allows evil to exist in the world
(Moses 7:26–33)

Sometimes our trials are not just natural disasters,
sickness, or untimely death. Sometimes they come as a
direct result of someone using agency to do evil. Ofttimes
when tragedy strikes, someone will say, "Well, it must
have been God's will." What exactly is "God's will"? It
seems to me that God's will, or God's desire, is that we
choose righteousness over wickedness! However, he also
desires that we have a choice in the matter. In the Pearl
of Great Price, Enoch sees a frightening vision: "And he
beheld Satan; and he had a great chain in his hand, and it
veiled the whole face of the earth with darkness; and he

looked up and laughed, and his angels rejoiced" (Moses 7:26).

In the scriptures, chains often symbolize bondage. Enoch sees Satan looking up and laughing at the world in chains, but Enoch also sees the Lord, who looks down on the sinful world and weeps. What a contrast! Satan looks up and laughs; God looks down and weeps. Enoch seems to be confused when he sees that God can cry, and he asks:

> How is it that the heavens weep, and shed forth their tears as the rain upon the mountains? And Enoch said unto the Lord: How is it that thou canst weep, seeing thou art holy, and from all eternity to all eternity? And were it possible that man could number the particles of the earth, yea, millions of earths like this, it would not be a beginning to the number of thy creations; and thy curtains are stretched out still; and yet thou art there, and thy bosom is there; and also thou art just; thou art merciful and kind forever. (Moses 7:28–30)

The Lord answers Enoch in what I think is one of the saddest passages of scripture in the standard works:

> The Lord said unto Enoch: Behold these thy brethren; they are the workmanship of

mine own hands, and I gave unto them their knowledge, in the day I created them; and in the Garden of Eden, gave I unto man his agency; and unto thy brethren have I said, and also given commandment, that they should love one another, and that they should choose me, their Father; but behold, they are without affection, and they hate their own blood. (Moses 7:32–33)

Clearly, "God's will," or what the Lord desires, is that we love one another and choose him. (Notice how similar this is to the two great commandments in Matthew 22:36–39: Love God and love your neighbor.) But some of God's children reject his will because "they are without affection, and they hate their own blood." Everyone on earth has agency, and sometimes those who misuse their agency have an impact on innocent people. This scripture from Moses provides evidence that the Lord notices the tragedies on earth and is affected by them.

President Boyd K. Packer once compared the plan of salvation to a three-act play. Act One, of course, is our premortal existence. Act Two is this life and is characterized by tests, trials, temptations, and tragedies. "Nowhere," said President Packer, "does the phrase 'happily ever after' appear in Act Two. That is reserved only for Act Three."

President Packer also counseled, "Do not suppose that God willfully causes that, which for his own purposes, he permits."[7] That statement is worth reading again: "Do not suppose that God willfully causes that, which for his own purposes, he permits." Obviously, there's an important difference between causing something to happen and allowing it to happen.

Did God cause the shooting at Columbine High School? No. Did he permit it? Yes. Did God cause the terrorist attacks of September 11, 2001? No. Did he permit them? Yes. God has given agency and freedom to his children, and many of them have used that agency in evil ways and made horrible choices. Elder Neal A. Maxwell taught:

> Throughout history the Stalins, Hitlers, and Herods have made their awful choices and performed their cruel works for an awful season. Clearly, while God is over all things, He does not do our choosing for us. Rather, the rule is, "Nevertheless, thou mayest choose for thyself" (Moses 3:17). Nor does He shield us from all the consequences of our bad choices. So much of our knowing the bitter and the

sweet consists of personally witnessing, if not experiencing, the consequences of both bad and good choices.[8]

We might conclude, then, that "God's will" is what God allows to happen.

There's another question in all of this that we haven't explored. How many terrorist attacks, school shootings, and other acts of premeditated evil has God prevented? We don't know. There's no way we could know. How many of these tragedies could have been much worse? Again, we don't know. The news media on the morning of September 11 estimated that about twenty thousand people could have been in the World Trade Center towers when the airplanes hit. The question "How could God allow this to happen?" was asked frequently that morning. Could it be that one day we'll discover that God prevented much more than he allowed? It's something to think about.

Closer to home, how many times has someone prayed that "we might get home in safety," and we actually did? How many traffic accidents has God helped you avoid? How many times has he protected your children when they were lost? How many times has he inspired you to do something that saved someone from injury? If God wants us to serve one another in anonymous ways, I suspect he may bless us and protect us without our knowledge as well.

The plan of happiness allows for the existence of agency and, therefore, evil. There is no flaw in the plan. Lehi taught, "For it must needs be, that there is an opposition in all things. If not so, my first-born in the wilderness, righteousness could not be brought to pass, neither wickedness, neither holiness nor misery, neither good nor bad" (2 Nephi 2:11).

We can rest assured that "all things have been done in the wisdom of him who knoweth all things" (2 Nephi 2:24). While we may not understand all the particulars, the Father's plan is perfect, and we were part of bringing it to pass. Elder Maxwell taught, "If we criticize God or are unduly miffed over sufferings and tribulation, we are really criticizing the Planner for implementing the very plan we once approved, premortally (see Job 38:4, 7). Granted, we don't remember the actual approval. But not remembering is actually part of the plan!"[9]

We can also rest assured that one day there will be an accounting. The Lord has made it clear how he feels about murderers and about those who would "offend one of these little ones" when he spoke of millstones and the depths of the sea (Matthew 18:6).

Scripture Two, the vision of Enoch, reminds us that God allows evil to exist in the world. We learn that God's will is that we choose him but that we have a choice in the first place. We also learn that the Lord is not unaffected by what happens here on earth. Enoch saw him weep!

SCRIPTURE THREE:
"Our work is not finished" (Alma 14:13)

Alma 14:13 was the first scripture that came to mind when I was preparing to speak to the young people at Columbine seminary. They needed a hero. They needed to look to someone who had witnessed a terrible tragedy, relied on Christ's atonement, and made it through. They needed Alma and Amulek.

As you recall, Alma and Amulek taught the people of Ammonihah, some of whom were of "the order and faith of Nehor" (Alma 14:16). The people of Ammonihah were so wicked that they responded by building a bonfire and throwing their scriptural records, along with the city's believing women and children, into the flames. They forced Alma and Amulek to watch the horrible suffering.

> And when Amulek saw the pains of the women and children who were consuming in the fire, he also was pained; and he said unto Alma: How can we witness this awful scene? Therefore let us stretch forth our hands, and

15

exercise the power of God which is in us, and
save them from the flames. (Alma 14:10)

"How can we witness this awful scene?" Many of us
have probably said something similar as we've watched
the news over the past several years. I wonder if any of
the students at Columbine High School had similar questions during the shooting. Alma answered: "The Spirit
constraineth me that I must not stretch forth mine hand;
for behold the Lord receiveth them up unto himself, in
glory" (Alma 14:11).

Those who believed in God were received unto him
in glory! They died, but they went to a glorious place. I
have recommended that many of my students cross reference Alma 14:11 to a comforting passage in the Doctrine
and Covenants: "And it shall come to pass that those that
die in me shall not taste of death, for it shall be sweet
unto them" (D&C 42:46).

Amulek then said to Alma, "Perhaps they will burn us
also" (Alma 14:12). Alma answered, "Be it according to
the will of the Lord. But, behold, our work is not finished;
therefore they burn us not" (Alma 14:13).

When I spoke to the youth at Columbine seminary, I
built my entire talk around Alma 14:13. I pled with them,
"Don't let this tragedy define your life! You still have your
own mission, your own patriarchal blessing, and your own

destiny, which is just yours! And like Alma and Amulek, perhaps you were spared because *your work is not finished!"*

The obvious question then becomes, what about those who die in such tragedies? Does that mean their work is finished? Perhaps, but there still remains much work to do in the spirit world. President Joseph Fielding Smith taught:

> May I say for the consolation of those who mourn, and for the comfort and guidance of all of us, that no righteous man is ever taken before his time. In the case of the faithful saints, they are simply transferred to other fields of labor. The Lord's work goes on in this life, in the world of spirits, and in the kingdoms of glory where men go after their resurrection.[10]

Again, we must go back to Scripture One and Nephi's response to the angel—we know God loves his children! We don't know why some people die and some people don't in tragedies. Many good people and many not-so-good people die every day. But we know God loves his children, in this life and in the next. Elder George Q. Morris taught: "Though the Lord condemns us to death—mortal death—it is one of the greatest blessings that comes to us here because it is the doorway to immortality, and we can never attain immortality without dying."[11]

Someone once said that the happiness of death is concealed from us so that we might better enjoy life. Death is just another milepost in the plan of salvation. President Spencer W. Kimball taught that "there is no tragedy in death, only in sin."[12] As I mentioned in the introduction, my father passed away as I began working on this book. A friend of mine who had been a mission president shared with me an insight from his experience about death. He noted the sadness experienced by families who send a missionary out into the field. He also observed the great joy experienced by the mission president and his wife as they welcome a new missionary into their area. The same event brings different feelings to different people, depending on where they are. Similarly, those who are left behind feel sadness at the passing of their loved one, but there is great joy in the spirit world as the departed spirit enters into the next phase of its eternal existence. President Brigham Young taught:

> We have more friends behind the veil than on this side, and they will hail us more joyfully than you were ever welcomed by your parents and friends in this world; and you will rejoice more when you meet them than you ever

rejoiced to see a friend in this life; and then we shall go on from step to step, from rejoicing to rejoicing, and from one intelligence and power to another, our happiness becoming more and more exquisite and sensible as we proceed in the words and powers of life.[13]

Sometimes death takes those who are in their youth or infancy. Those of us who remain find the loss particularly difficult when it is untimely. The Prophet Joseph Smith taught that while we may mourn for those who die while still young, we mourn with an eternal perspective:

The Lord takes many away even in infancy, that they may escape the envy of man, and the sorrows and evils of this present world; they were too pure, too lovely, to live on earth; therefore if rightly considered, instead of mourning we have reason to rejoice as they are delivered from evil, and we shall soon have them again. . . . The only difference between the old and young dying is, one lives longer in heaven and eternal light and glory than the other, and is freed a little sooner from this miserable, wicked world. Notwithstanding all this glory, we for a moment lose sight of it, and mourn the loss, but we do not mourn as those without hope.[14]

Sadly, many people feel such hopelessness that they decide to take their own lives. But suicide doesn't solve any problems; it just changes the venue. Because only the Lord really knows what was going on in the mind and heart of someone who has taken his own life, we still have reason to hope. Elder Bruce R. McConkie has written:

> Suicide consists in the voluntary and intentional taking of one's own life, particularly where the person involved is accountable and has a sound mind. . . . Persons subject to great stresses may lose control of themselves and become mentally clouded to the point that they are no longer accountable for their acts. Such are not to be condemned for taking their own lives. It should be remembered that judgment is the Lord's; he knows the thoughts, intents, and abilities of men; and he in his infinite wisdom will make all things right in due course.[15]

The best way to prepare for death is to live life to its fullest. I believe the Lord will hold us accountable for what we do with our lives, whether they are easy or whether they are filled with trials. Alma and Amulek had to go on, and so do we. I believe it is safe to say that if we are still here, "Our work is not finished."

Alma and Amulek witnessed an awful scene. I wonder if they ever forgot what they saw. I suspect they had many nightmares, as the young people at Columbine did. How did they survive? The answer lies in Scripture Four.

SCRIPTURE FOUR:
The Atonement is not just for sinners (Alma 7:11–12)

We know that Jesus died for our sins. We know that he suffered for the things that we do wrong, and if we repent we will not need to suffer. But Scripture Four teaches us that Jesus not only suffered for the things we do wrong but also for the things that happen *to* us—things over which we have no control. Alma taught the people of Gideon:

> And he [the Son of God] shall go forth, suffering pains and afflictions and temptations of every kind; and this that the word might be fulfilled which saith he will take upon him the pains and the sicknesses of his people. And he will take upon him death, that he may loose the bands of death which bind his people; and he will take upon him their infirmities, that his bowels may be filled with mercy, according to

21

Reference	Age	Event
Mormon 2:2	15	Mormon leads Nephite armies against Lamanites
Mormon 2:9	19	Nephites are attacked by an army of 44,000
Mormon 2:15	33	Thousands are "hewn down in open rebellion against their God"
Mormon 2:22	35	Nephites are attacked again
Mormon 2:28	39	Nephites retake lands and make a treaty with the Lamanites
Mormon 3:7	50	Lamanites attack the city of Desolation
Mormon 3:8	51	Lamanites come down to battle again
Mormon 4:1	52	Nephites attack Lamanites
Mormon 4:7	53	Lamanites attack city of Teancum
Mormon 4:15	56	Nephites attack Lamanites
Mormon 4:16–17	64	Innumerable army of Lamanites attacks
Mormon 5:6	69	Lamanites attack again
Mormon 6:5	73	Nephites gather at Cumorah for tremendous battle

the flesh, that he may know according to the
flesh how to succor his people according to
their infirmities. (Alma 7:11–12)

The word "sin" does not appear anywhere in those
two verses. But notice the other words—the things in
addition to sins that Jesus took upon him: *pains, afflictions,
temptations, sicknesses, infirmities,* and *death.* Alma and Amulek
must have relied on the Atonement to get them through
the sadness, the nightmares, and the emotional trauma of
the events in Ammonihah, and we must rely on the
Atonement to help us through our personal tragedies as
well.

While serving on an aircraft carrier in World War II,
my father survived a kamikaze attack near Iwo Jima
toward the end of the war. His two years in the service
had a great impact on him. If two years can affect someone so deeply, what would happen to someone who spent
nearly his entire life at war? Would that person become
hardened, bitter, and resentful? Not necessarily, as illus-
trated by the life of the prophet Mormon. Mormon took
over the Nephite armies at fifteen and fought until he was
at least seventy-three, as the chart at left shows.

Within a span of fifty-eight years, Mormon fought in
several major battles and witnessed the death of tens of
thousands of his people! Yet he was filled not with hate
and bitterness but with the pure love of Christ. Try to

23

imagine a large, powerful, battle-hardened career general standing up in testimony meeting and saying this:

> Charity is the pure love of Christ, and it endureth forever; and whoso is found possessed of it at the last day, it shall be well with him. Wherefore, my beloved brethren, pray unto the Father with all the energy of heart, that ye may be filled with this love, which he hath bestowed upon all who are true followers of his Son, Jesus Christ; that ye may become the sons of God; that when he shall appear we shall be like him, for we shall see him as he is; that we may have this hope; that we may be purified even as he is pure. Amen. (Moroni 7:47–48)

How did Mormon manage to keep his spiritual sensitivity while growing up in an environment of war? He must have been renewed by the Atonement, which can take away not only the pain of our sins but also the pain of things that happen to us over which we have no control (Alma 7:11).

Is the Atonement powerful enough to help someone who has suffered physical or sexual abuse? Absolutely. The atonement of Jesus Christ is infinite and eternal. Dr. Carlfred Broderick, a Latter-day Saint and noted family counselor, related the story of a woman who had endured such abuse. On one occasion, she asked Dr. Broderick a tough question that evoked an inspired answer:

> "Where is the justice? How can God pretend to be just and send some little girls into homes where they are loved . . . and made to feel like somebody and others into homes where they are beat and molested and abused and neglected? What did I do in the pre-earth life to deserve such a family?" I felt inspired at that time to tell her that she had volunteered in the preexistence to be a savior on Mount Zion, to come to a family drowning in sickness and sin and to be the means of purifying that lineage. Before her in that line were generations of ugly, destructive, family relationships. Downstream from her purifying influence every generation would be blessed with light and love. The role of a savior, I said, is to suffer innocently for the sins of others that still others may not suffer. There can be no higher calling.[16]

This woman had suffered abuse as a child, but the Atonement gave her the power to refuse to pass it on. It's hard to imagine a greater evil that could be done to a child. The impact of such an evil would require a power greater than the evil to bring peace and healing. The greatest power available is the atonement of Jesus Christ. Christ suffered not only for our sins but also for the bad things that happen to us.

SCRIPTURE FIVE:
One day the Lord will reveal all things (D&C 101:32–36)

We may never have all of the answers in this life. The newspapers, the cable news networks, and the politicians will be debating the causes and solutions to our modern problems for years to come. We must look for our answers in books where the answers don't change. One day the Lord will return and answer all of our questions: "Yea, verily I say unto you, in that day when the Lord shall come, he shall reveal all things—Things which have passed, and hidden things which no man knew, things of the earth, by which it was made, and the purpose and the end thereof" (D&C 101:32–33).

Imagine all of the areas of science we could list under the heading "Things which have passed." How about archaeology, anthropology, and geology, just to name a few? Next, look at the phrase "hidden things which no man knew." Take today's greatest scientists, give them an unlimited budget, a state-of-the-art laboratory, unlimited resources, and no time limit! Then ask them to create one mosquito. Sometimes we think we're so smart! But Jesus will reveal "hidden things which no man knew."

Think of the perplexing questions regarding the big bang, evolution, and the age of the dinosaur. How old is the earth? How old is matter? If you bake a cake using eggs that are two days old, milk that is one week old, flour that is six months old and sugar that is one year old, how old is the cake?

Scripture Five assures us that one day the Lord will reveal "things of the earth, by which it was made, and the purpose and the end thereof." But that's not all! The list continues:

> Things most precious, things that are above, and things that are beneath, things that are in the earth, and upon the earth, and in heaven. And all they who suffer persecution for my name, and endure in faith, though they are called to lay down their lives for my sake yet shall they partake of all this glory. Wherefore, fear not even unto death; for in this world your joy is not full, but in me your joy is full. (D&C 101:34–36)

Indeed, this world is Act Two—a series of tests, trials, temptations, and sometimes even tragedies, but in Christ our joy is full.

You may have noticed a qualifier in the title of this chapter: "Five Scriptures That Will Help You Get through *Almost* Anything." Ultimately, it is not the scriptures that help us get through things but the Lord Jesus Christ, of whom the scriptures testify, who helps us through. He is the one who will help us get through *anything* and *everything*. Because of Jesus Christ, we can remove the word "almost." Jesus didn't *almost* conquer death and hell, he conquered it. Jesus didn't *almost* accomplish the infinite and eternal Atonement, he accomplished it. The language of the scriptures is absolute when it comes to the power of the Savior. Notice the absence of the word "almost" in the following verses:

- D&C 88:6—Jesus descended below *all* things.
- Alma 7:11—He suffered temptations of *every* kind.
- Hebrews 4:15—He was tempted in "*all* points . . . as we are, yet without sin."
- D&C 58:22—He will subdue *all* enemies under his feet.
- D&C 50:41—He overcame the world.
- John 1:3—"*All* things were made by him."
- D&C 50:27—"*All* things are subject unto him."
- D&C 88:41—He comprehends *all* things.
- D&C 101:16—*All* flesh is in his hands.
- John 14:26—Through the Holy Ghost, he will bring *all* things to our remembrance.

- Matthew 19:26—He taught that "with God *all* things are possible."
- Romans 8:28—Because of him, *all* things that we experience will work together for our good.

Finally, and most important in relation to this discussion, in the midst of our trials and adversity, he promises us the power to overcome "all things" with no "almost": "By giving heed and doing these things which ye have received, and which ye shall hereafter receive . . . the kingdom is given you of the Father, and *power to overcome all things*" (D&C 50:35; emphasis added).

That's not a crutch. That's a sword.

Scripture Five attests that Jesus is the Master Teacher who has a Teacher's Edition with all of the answers. While we may not have all of the answers in this life, the Lord does, and we can trust him more than anyone or anything in this world. He will help us get through *everything*.

CONCLUSION

These five scriptures give us is an eternal perspective. "Eternal perspective" is a phrase used so often that it may have lost some of its meaning. I hope not. When our spirit sees with an eternal perspective, we become aware that we need not fear *anything*. We know where we came from, we know why we're here, and we know what will ultimately happen when we leave this life.

Some things in life are temporary, and some are permanent. Our temporal life is temporary. Our trials are temporary. Our pain is temporary. Because of the Savior and his atonement, our mortality will become immortality, and we may dwell with God in a state of permanent, or "never-ending happiness" (Mosiah 2:41). President Howard W. Hunter taught, "Please remember this one thing. If our lives and our faith are centered upon Jesus Christ and his restored gospel, nothing can ever go permanently wrong. On the other hand, if our lives are not centered on the Savior and his teachings, no other success can ever be permanently right."[17]

We know that the Lord will be victorious and that his victory will be permanent. That very thought should give us faith and hope. Elder Jeffrey R. Holland has observed:

> The future of this world has long been declared; the final outcome between good and evil is already known. There is absolutely no question as to who wins because the victory has already been posted on the scoreboard. The only really strange thing in all of this is that we are still down here on the field trying to decide which team's jersey we want to wear![18]

Those who have done needlepoint know it's important which side of the fabric to display. One side is full of crisscrossing threads and tiny knots that make the design difficult to recognize. But when it's turned over, the entire picture comes into view. I have always loved the following poem about a needlepoint or weaving design. It helps me trust God when I can't understand why things happen the way they do.

> *My life is but a weaving between my God and me;*
> *I cannot choose the colors He worketh steadily.*
> *Ofttimes He weaveth sorrow, and I in foolish pride,*
> *Forget that He seeth the upper, and I the under side.*
> *Not till the loom is silent and the shuttles cease to fly,*
> *Shall God unroll the canvas and explain the reason why.*
> *The dark threads are as needful in the Weaver's skillful hand,*
> *As the threads of gold and silver in the pattern He has planned.*[19]

Someone once said that in this life suffering is mandatory, but misery is optional. No one's going to make it out of here alive. We're all going to pass through some trials and perhaps even some tragedies.

But what do we know for sure, from a source whose answers don't change? We know that God loves his children (1 Nephi 11:17). We know that part of his plan is to allow evil to exist in the world and that he is not unaffected by what happens here on earth (Moses 7:26–33). We know that if we're still alive, we have a work to accomplish (Alma 14:13). We know that the Savior suffered not only for our sins but also for our pains and afflictions (Alma 7:11–12). And we know that one day the Lord will conquer the evil one, answer all of our questions, and bless us with a fulness of joy (D&C 101:32-36).

NOTES

1. Richard G. Scott, "Trust in the Lord," *Ensign*, November 1995, 16.

2. Truman G. Madsen, *Joseph Smith the Prophet* (Salt Lake City: Bookcraft, 1989), 93.

3. George Q. Cannon, in Conference Reports of The Church of Jesus Christ of Latter-day Saints (Salt Lake City: The Church of Jesus Christ of Latter-day Saints, 1898 to present), April 1899, 66.

4. Orson F. Whitney, in Spencer W. Kimball, *Faith Precedes the Miracle* (Salt Lake City: Deseret Book, 1972), 98.

5. Neal A. Maxwell, "Lest Ye Be Wearied and Faint in Your Minds," *Ensign*, May 1991, 88.

6. George Q. Cannon, in Neal A. Maxwell, *If Thou Endure It Well* (Salt Lake City: Bookcraft, 1996), 121.

7. Boyd K. Packer, "The Play and the Plan," Church Educational System Devotional, 7 May 1995, 3.

8. Neal A. Maxwell, *That Ye May Believe* (Salt Lake City: Bookcraft, 1992), 29.

9. Ibid., 10.

10. Joseph Fielding Smith, in Robert L. Millet and Joseph Fielding McConkie, *The Life Beyond* (Salt Lake City: Bookcraft, 1986), vii.

11. George Q. Morris, in Conference Report, April 1958, 39.

12. Spencer W. Kimball, *The Teachings of Spencer W. Kimball,* ed. Edward L. Kimball (Salt Lake City: Bookcraft, 1982), 39.

13. Brigham Young, *Discourses of Brigham Young,* sel. John A. Widtsoe (Salt Lake City: Deseret Book, 1954), 379–80.

14. Joseph Smith, *Teachings of the Prophet Joseph Smith,* sel. Joseph Fielding Smith (Salt Lake City: Deseret Book, 1976), 196–97.

15. Bruce R. McConkie, *Mormon Doctrine,* 2d ed. (Salt Lake City: Bookcraft, 1966), 771.

16. Carlfred Broderick, *One Flesh, One Heart* (Salt Lake City: Deseret Book, 1986), 52.

17. Howard W. Hunter, "'Fear Not, Little Flock,'" *Brigham Young University 1988–89 Devotional and Fireside Speeches* (Provo, Utah: University Publications, 1989), 112.

18. E-mail correspondence from Jeffrey R. Holland to John Bytheway, 1 June 2004.

19. "The Weaver," in *Sourcebook of Poetry,* comp. Al Bryant (Grand Rapids, Mich: Zondervan Publishing House, 1968), 664.

Chapter Two

Five Scriptures That Will Strengthen Your Marriage

President Harold B. Lee made a prophetic statement in 1972: "Satan's greatest threat today is to destroy the family, and to make a mockery of the law of chastity and the sanctity of the marriage covenant."[1]

In 1972, the shows on prime-time television may have been empty and inane, but they weren't obscene. Things changed in a hurry, however. In 1976, the average prime-time television show contained two sexual references per hour. That number doubled to four sexual references per hour of prime-time in 1986. Ten years later, the number of sexual references jumped to eight and a half per hour. If the trend holds, the number of sexual references per hour of prime-time in 2006 will be about seventeen.[2] While these numbers have been climbing, references to virtues such as commitment, loyalty, chastity, and virtue have become noticeably absent.

Things aren't much better at the movie theater. The average R-rated movie in 1992 portrayed sex outside of marriage more than sex within marriage by an astonishing ratio of 36 to 1![3] If that isn't a perfect example of mocking the law of chastity and the sanctity of the marriage covenant, I don't know what is. Indeed, as the song says, "The truths and values we embrace are mocked on every hand,"[4] and on every screen and picture tube.

Twenty-three years after President Lee's statement, President Gordon B. Hinckley announced a proclamation to the world on the family, restating and reinforcing the sacredness of chastity, the sanctified roles of men and women, and the divinely ordained marriage covenant.[5] Now more than ever, we must draw on scriptural power to reaffirm the importance of chastity and to strengthen our marriages.

SCRIPTURE ONE:

"Remember the covenant wherewith ye have covenanted one with another" (D&C 90:24)

This verse has become an important motto in my marriage. Kim and I have found it to be so important and useful that we've displayed it in a place of prominence in our home—a place where it will be seen daily, a place where others may view it and witness our commitment to one another, a place of comings and goings, a place of family gatherings, a place of supreme and singular importance—on the fridge!

Joking aside, we have applied the phrase "Remember the covenant" to our marriage covenant. When we remember the covenant, we quickly see things in their proper perspective. With the big picture in view, we can reduce what we might initially see as large problems to little things that we can usually easily solve. There is a monumental difference between a *contract* and a *covenant.* When we struggle to make decisions that affect our marriage—and almost every decision does—our first and best strategy is to remember our covenants.

Sometimes our contract relationships cause problems with our covenant relationships. For example, on occasion I have to remind myself that I have not made a covenant with ESPN. I have not made a covenant with the golf course. I have not made a covenant with college football or the NBA (although it might appear so when the Jazz make the playoffs). I have not made a covenant with the Internet, computer games, cable TV, or any other form of recreation. A million distractions can pull us away from our covenant obligations if we're not "remembering."

My brothers and sisters (all of whom are now married and have families of their own) are some of my best friends in the world, but I have not made a covenant with them. Nor have I made a covenant with my in-laws. My covenant is with my wife, and hers is with me. We are a new family, our own family unit, and that is where our priority must remain.

The bottom line is that if I left my heart with the San Francisco 49ers, my heart is in the wrong place. The Lord declared, "Thou shalt love thy wife with all thy heart, and shalt cleave unto her and none else" (D&C 42:22). That's part of my covenant.

My marriage thrives when Kim and I remember our covenant to each other. It's incredibly affirming to have a wife who makes me feel that I'm first in her life, who hangs up the phone when I walk in, and who understands that I like to have time alone with her each day. (It's sad when, after a long day of work, a husband is greeted with more excitement by the dog than by the one with whom he has made and received covenants.)

Those who honor their covenant marriages approach problems with a greater determination to make their covenants fruitful. Elder Bruce C. Hafen has taught:

> When troubles come, the parties to a *contractual* marriage seek happiness by walking away. They marry to obtain benefits and will stay only as long as they're receiving what

they bargained for. But when troubles come to a *covenant* marriage, the husband and wife work them through. They marry to give and to grow, bound by covenants to each other, to the community, and to God. *Contract* companions each give 50 percent; *covenant* companions each give 100 percent.

Marriage is by nature a covenant, not just a private contract one may cancel at will. Jesus taught about contractual attitudes when he described the "hireling" who performs his conditional promise of care only when he receives something in return. When the hireling "seeth the wolf coming," he "leaveth the sheep, and fleeth . . . because he . . . careth not for the sheep." By contrast, the Savior said, "I am the good shepherd, . . . and I lay down my life for the sheep" (John 10:12–15). Many people today marry as hirelings. And when the wolf comes, they flee. This idea is wrong. It curses the earth, turning parents' hearts away from their children and from each other (D&C 2).[6]

Covenant marriages have access to the infinite power of God because God is the third party in the covenant relationship. He's on our side, and he will never fail to keep his part of the covenant! His work and his glory is to bring to pass our immortality and eternal life, and that will only happen if we, as the other two parties, keep our covenants. Therefore, because God wants us to keep our covenants, we know that he will prepare a way for us to do the things he commands.

It's important to remember that anyone who receives salvation and exaltation will receive it by covenant. God works with his children by covenants. Baptism is a covenant, and marriage is a covenant. The Book of Mormon teaches that many things that were "plain and most precious" were taken away from the gospel of the Lamb. We generally think of certain doctrines being removed from the scriptures when we hear the phrase "plain and precious things," but the rest of the verse identifies another vital element of the gospel that was removed: "and also many covenants of the Lord have they taken away" (1 Nephi 13:26). The gospel is referred to as "restored" because it restored covenants—enriching, exalting, marriage-blessing covenants.

As we grow older and our schedules grow more hectic, one of the questions we often ask ourselves is, "What are my priorities?" To answer that question, I suggest we ask, "With whom have I made covenants?" We can discover our greatest priorities simply by remembering our most important covenants.

Every time Kim and I approach the fridge, Scripture One reminds us to "remember our covenants," and it gives an eternal perspective to a marriage that unfolds one day at a time.

SCRIPTURE TWO:
"Is it I?" (Matthew 26:22)

Shortly after the Savior retired with the Twelve to eat the Last Supper, he stunned the disciples with the words, "One of you shall betray me." Their reaction was one of meekness and self-examination. Matthew records, "They were exceeding sorrowful, and began every one of them to say unto him, Lord, is it I?" (Matthew 26:21–22).

The question "Is it I?" looks inward. It is an outward recognition of an inner weakness. It says, "I may have done something wrong. Will you help me to know if I have?"

When Jesus said, "One of you shall betray me," the disciples did *not* respond, "I'll bet it's him." Sadly, many marriage problems are articulated in exactly that manner. "It's my *spouse's* fault. It's my *spouse* who needs to change. I'm the normal one. It is *not* I."

Scripture Two, when applied to a marriage relationship, is a valuable tool for creating an environment in which problems can be talked about and solved. Marriage partners can ask themselves the same question, early and often: "Did I do something wrong?" "Have I hurt your feelings in some way?" "Is there something I can do better?" The words themselves are not as important as the meekness required of the one who does the asking.

If someone were to ask whether communication skills or meekness is most important to a marriage, I'd answer meekness, hands down. You can be a superb communicator but still never have the humility to ask, "Is it I?" *Communication skills are no substitute for Christlike attributes.* As Dr. Douglas Brinley has observed, "Without . . . theological perspectives, . . . secular exercises designed to improve our relationship and our communication skills (the common tools of counselors and marriage books) will never work any permanent change in one's heart: *they simply develop more clever and skilled fighters!*"[7]

An illustration of meekness in marriage can be found early in the Book of Mormon. Father Lehi sent his sons back to Jerusalem to retrieve the brass plates from Laban—a powerful man who didn't want to give them up. Sariah was understandably concerned. Nephi reported that she "complained against my father, telling him that he was a visionary man; saying: Behold thou hast led us forth from the land of our inheritance, and my sons are no more, and we perish in the wilderness" (1 Nephi 5:2).

Lehi could have responded in a number of ways. He could have said, "You have no idea what you're talking about," or "Don't you believe in me?" or "Where's your faith?" But he didn't. He agreed with her! "I know that I am a visionary man; for if I had not seen the things of God in a vision I should not have known the goodness of God, but had tarried at Jerusalem, and had perished with my brethren" (1 Nephi 5:4).

Lehi listened to Sariah and reassured her with his testimony that their sons would return. "And after this manner of language did my father, Lehi, comfort my mother, Sariah" (1 Nephi 5:6).

Did Lehi take a class in communication skills before he packed up the family and left? I doubt it. They seemed to be in quite a hurry to get out of Jerusalem. But Lehi possessed the Christlike attribute of meekness, and his response to Sariah has helped me in my marriage. He listened to Sariah's feelings and then spoke reassuring words of comfort.

My wife and I call this "listen before logic," or "feelings before facts." As a husband (and as a male who has assumed that my role is to fix whatever is broken), I have often been tempted to skip to the solution without acknowledging the emotions. Not any more. Now I listen as intently as I can until my wife knows that her feelings are understood and respected. Then, and only then, can I go into fix-it mode and say, "Let's think about what we can do about this."

When meekness is present, miracles can happen. One marriage counselor observed, "I have learned over the years that if I can ever get a couple to apologize to each other, the other problems seem to melt away."[8] The "Is it I?" attitude creates a setting where the Spirit may dwell, where there is no shouting, no blaming, and no resentment. In that humble atmosphere, as we "remember the covenant wherewith [we] have covenanted one with another" (D&C 90:24), our problems are more easily and more calmly addressed and solved.

SCRIPTURE THREE:
"For which of you, intending to build a tower, sitteth not down first, and counteth the cost. . . ?" (Luke 14:28)

Scripture Three can be applied to almost any area of life. Parents wish their teenagers would use it more often. It requires not only looking at decisions but also examining their consequences. Those who do not sit down first and count the cost are often left with an unfinished tower. The same idea is expressed in the old saying, "If you fail to plan, you plan to fail."

Unfortunately, most couples spend more time planning the wedding than planning the marriage. The wedding is a piece of cake—literally and figuratively, featuring a daylong party with photos, family, fun, and food (and no kids).

The marriage, on the other hand, is something else—a fifty- to eighty-year commitment with adjustments, apartments, bills, accidents, budgets, mortgages, stress, spats, credit limits, babies, vaccinations, overdrafts, sickness, diapers, soccer, sitters, spills, bandages, floods, groceries, minivans, debt, teenagers, dating, driving, proms, heartbreaks, callings, curfews, graduations, tuition, missions, farewells, homecomings, more marriages, grandchildren, unexpected visits, loans, babysitting, uninvited (but welcome) dinner guests, and on and on.

Weddings are fun and honeymoons are awesome, but they are temporary. Marriages are permanent (we hope), and to make a marriage work, both partners better sit down and count the cost. As someone wisely observed, "Whatever we obtain, we have to maintain." Counting the cost of building a tower includes planning for the maintenance of that tower. Without attention, the tower will eventually crumble and fall apart. Once it's built, it must be maintained.

Whenever I see the word *maintenance,* I always think of cars. My dad was a master at maintaining cars. Our family drove an embarrassingly homely 1964 Dodge Polara throughout my high school years. We put more than 230,000 miles on that heap before my father finally sold it. Every single Saturday, Dad would disappear into the garage, where he would raise the hoods and check the fluid levels on all of our vehicles. It was a ritual with him. Dad taught me that you can ruin a new car in a matter of months if you don't maintain it. On the other hand, with a little regular maintenance, you can keep a car running smoothly for decades—even a light green '64 Dodge that your kids can't stand.

Similarly, a marriage can last for decades and into eternity if it's well maintained. So, to paraphrase a popular saying, "Ask not what your marriage can do for you, ask what you can do for your marriage."

You may remember that in teaching the Zoramites how to grow and maintain their testimonies of Christ, Alma compared "the word unto a seed" (Alma 32:28). I know a wise bishop who counseled couples to read Alma's teachings in Alma 32:37–41 and replace the words "seed," "tree," and "word" with the word "marriage." Notice how nicely it fits:

> And behold, as the *marriage* beginneth to grow, ye will say: Let us nourish it with great care, that it may get root, that it may grow up, and bring forth fruit unto us. And now behold, if ye nourish it with much care it will get root, and grow up, and bring forth fruit.

But if ye neglect the *marriage*, and take no thought for its nourishment, behold it will not get any root; and when the heat of the sun cometh and scorcheth it, because it hath no root it withers away, and ye pluck it up and cast it out.

Now, this is not because the *marriage* was not good, neither is it because the fruit thereof would not be desirable; but it is because your ground is barren, and ye will not nourish the *marriage*, therefore ye cannot have the fruit thereof.

And thus, if ye will not nourish the *marriage*, looking forward with an eye of faith to the fruit thereof, ye can never pluck of the fruit of the tree of life.

But if ye will nourish the *marriage*, yea, nourish the *marriage* as it beginneth to grow, by your faith with great diligence, and with patience, looking forward to the fruit thereof, it shall take root; and behold it shall be a *marriage* springing up unto everlasting life.

Maintaining a marriage can be as simple as asking a few questions of one another on a weekly basis. In my marriage, the routine for asking these questions is not as precise as regularly scheduled auto maintenance ("Please check your marriage every three months or three thousand disagreements, whichever comes first"), but it is fairly regular. The questions we often ask one another are: "How do you feel about things?" "Am I being a good husband/ wife?" "Is there anything I could do better?"

Kim and I, and probably every other couple, enjoy getting away. When our anniversary comes, we hire a sitter and we disappear. We love our time together, and we always set aside a portion of our getaway to "count the cost." How are we doing? We were married in the temple, but is our marriage celestial? Are we growing together or growing apart? How's our budget, our temple attendance, our scripture study, our family home evening, and our spiritual well-being? What can we do better in the coming year?

For us, it all comes down to a slight adaptation of Luke 14:28: "For which of you, intending to build a celestial marriage, sitteth not down first (and on every weekend and subsequent anniversary), and counteth the cost?" Part of marriage is maintenance, and maintenance makes a marriage last.

SCRIPTURE FOUR:
"He who has repented of his sins, the same is forgiven, and I, the Lord, remember them no more" (D&C 58:42)

This scripture is a great source of hope and a testimony of the Lord's mercy. It illustrates that through repentance, the Lord is willing to "forgive and forget" and allow us to enjoy fellowship with him despite past transgressions. This verse can also bless our marriages because if we are genuinely "trying to be like Jesus," we will develop a forgiving disposition.

The fact is, we *must* forgive in order to receive forgiveness. In the Sermon on the Mount, the Lord taught, "For if ye forgive men their trespasses, your heavenly Father will also forgive you: But if ye forgive not men their trespasses, neither will your Father forgive your trespasses" (Matthew 6:14–15). Additionally, the Lord's Prayer teaches that we should ask God to "forgive us our debts, as we forgive our debtors" (Matthew 6:12).

One of my wife's greatest traits—one that I knew very little about the day we got married—is how quickly she forgives. In fact, she forgives and forgets almost instantly, and in such cases I'm always motivated to be a better husband.

I believe the phrase "and I, the Lord, remember them no more" is poetic. I suspect that the Lord doesn't literally forget our sins but that the phrase "remember them no more" is a poetic way of saying that they will not be "remembered" or "mentioned" at the Judgment (Ezekiel 18:22). Similarly, we will probably remember many things our spouse has done that caused hurt feelings but for which we received an apology. Once our spouse has asked forgiveness, our goal is to do as the Lord has promised and "remember them no more."

The temptation to rewind, replay, and rehash past mistakes only leads to resentment. Unfortunately, some spouses keep a mental database of their partner's past sins and continue to bring them up at certain times, as if the former apology had never been offered and the forgiveness never really given. This cycle damages the relationship, and it implies that former efforts to apologize were meaningless. We would never want to send that kind of message to the person with whom we have made covenants.

During my honeymoon, I told my wife that if I ever hurt her feelings, she could *know*, with an absolute certainty, that I didn't do it on purpose. I promised that I would never intentionally make her feel bad, and she promised me the same. What kind of Melchizedek Priesthood holder would deliberately cause his wife pain? "Amen to the priesthood . . . of that man" (D&C 121:37).

After nine years of marriage, we can honestly say that our honeymoon agreement has worked beautifully. Make no mistake, we have hurt each other's feelings on many occasions, but we have never done it on purpose. We're striving to "remember the covenant wherewith [we] have covenanted one with another," and we have too much respect and admiration for each other to deliberately cause each other pain.

The spirit of love and forgiveness can help us overlook our spouse's quirks and foibles. I've learned a great lesson from King Lamoni's wife about overlooking little things. After Ammon had taught the Lamanite king about the Creation, the Fall, and the Atonement, King Lamoni began to pray for mercy. He soon fell to the earth, unconscious. Later, King Lamoni's wife told Ammon, "Some say that he is not dead, but others say that he is dead and that he stinketh, and that he ought to be placed in the sepulchre; but as for myself, to me he doth not stink" (Alma 19:5).

I'm grateful that my wife, like the wife of Lamoni, overlooks so many of my faults, even those that are fairly obvious to others. In effect, she says, "Some say that my husband is dense and a simpleton, but as for myself, to me he is not so dumb." Because my wife overlooks my foibles, I try to do the same kind of overlooking as well.

Perhaps no one in the world knows our weaknesses as well as our spouses, which is precisely why we need a humble and forgiving attitude. James taught, "Confess your faults one to another, and pray for one another, that ye may be healed" (James 5:16). I'm convinced that the Lord smiles on married couples who strive to keep their covenants, confess their faults to each other, pray for one another, and, as Scripture Four suggests, remember each other's sins no more.

SCRIPTURE FIVE:
"Better is a dinner of herbs where love is, than a stalled ox and hatred therewith" (Proverbs 15:17)

I chose this scripture because it shows us that some priorities are more important than others, period. This verse helps me to see that no matter what else is going on, we ought to have the spirit of love, acceptance, and peace in our marriage. We can reword this verse a thousand ways and apply the priorities that really matter in our own homes. For example:

"Better is an apartment where the Spirit is, than a great and spacious mansion and hatred therewith."

"Better is a beat-up minivan where financial security is, than four BMWs and indebtedness therewith."

"Better is a toothpaste tube squeezed in the middle where love is, than a perfectly squeezed toothpaste tube and hatred therewith."

Some things are simply not worth fighting about. Winning an argument about the toothpaste, the toilet seat, or a messy bathroom is not worth the loss of the Spirit. I am unaware of any scripture that tells us how to dispense toothpaste, but I am aware of many that teach us to have love in our marriages and families. Why? Because the spirit of contention is the spirit of the devil (3 Nephi 11:29). The priority we must strive for is to always have the Spirit of the Lord in our homes.

We can still have a discussion about toothpaste dispensing, toilet seats, and clutter in the bathroom, but we must talk with sensitivity and patience, thus allowing the Spirit to remain with us. What could be better than that?

Kim and I recently listened to an audio program that had a profound effect on us. Dr. Wendy L. Watson, a professor of marriage and family therapy at Brigham Young University, tried an experiment with eight women, ages eighteen to fifty-five. She asked them to do something simple but specific for five days (I'll tell you what in a moment). "The experiences of these women," Dr. Watson reported, "blew us all away." Among the results they experienced were:

- An increased desire to "de-junk" their physical environments.
- A greatly reduced desire to watch TV.
- An increased desire to reach out to others and follow through on commitments.
- An increased ability to be kinder, gentler, and more patient.
- An increased desire to take care of their bodies by living the Lord's law of health more fully.

- An increased ability to see how they could have handled situations better.
- An increased mental focus.
- An increased ability and desire to study and learn.
- A greatly decreased desire to backbite, gossip, or be cynical.
- A dramatic increase in their physical energy because energy-draining negative emotions were gone.
- An unbelievable reduction in stress.
- Profound changes in their conversations with others.

Dr. Watson continued for several minutes, detailing more of the achievements of these women. By now you're probably asking, "What in the world did they do? How could someone possibly make all those changes in their lives? Did they read some kind of motivational book? Did they hire a personal success coach for $700 an hour? Did they take herbal supplements or some kind of wonder drug?"

No. All they did was rely on something they already possessed. Here's the experiment Dr. Watson asked them to perform:

> For five days in their morning prayers,
> they were to pray with concerted effort for the

Holy Ghost to be with them that day. Then, throughout the day, as they encountered any difficult, tempting, or trying situation, they were to pray for and really picture the Spirit being right there with them.[9]

My wife and I were astounded as we listened to the results. Later, lying in bed and staring at the ceiling, I found myself feeling a little foolish and saying to myself, "Of course, that's true. Of course it is." Heavenly Father gave us a gift so priceless that the Doctrine and Covenants calls it "the unspeakable gift of the Holy Ghost" (D&C 121:26). We all have it, but perhaps we haven't been striving to keep it with us, really listening and acting on what it tells us to do.

It dawned on me that evening that *the greatest success formula ever devised is repeated every Sunday by sixteen-year-old boys.* If we are willing to take upon us the name of Christ, and always remember him, and keep his commandments which he has given us, we can *always have his spirit to be with us!*

No motivational book, no personal success coach, no herbal supplement, new diet or exercise machine could ever hope to match the power of having a member of the Godhead with us 24/7. As stated in the introduction, the gospel of Jesus Christ is not a crutch for the weak-minded, it's the sword of the Spirit for the spiritually minded, giving us victory over the world and peace in our homes.

CONCLUSION

I suggest that the greatest key to strengthening our marriages is to keep the Holy Ghost with us. I would rather have the Spirit in my marriage than have every possible material blessing and be without the Spirit (Proverbs 15:17). With that goal in mind, we're motivated to "remember the covenant" we've made with each other (D&C 90:24), to have an "Is it I?" (Matthew 26:22) attitude when problems arise (Luke 14:78), to maintain our marriage well beyond the wedding, and to keep the spirit of forgiveness by remembering our spouse's sins and foibles "no more" (D&C 58:42).

NOTES

1. Harold B. Lee, *The Teachings of Harold B. Lee*, ed. Clyde J. Williams (Salt Lake City: Bookcraft, 1996), 227.

2. "A Family Affair," *Primetime Live*, first aired 11 December 1996.

3. Randal A. Wright, *Why Do Good People See Bad Movies?* (Provo, Utah: National Family Institute, 1993), 81.

4. "As Zion's Youth in Latter Days," *Hymns of The Church of Jesus Christ of Latter-day Saints* (Salt Lake City: The Church of Jesus Christ of Latter-day Saints, 1985), no. 256.

5. "The Family: A Proclamation to the World," *Ensign*, November 1995, 102.

6. Bruce C. Hafen, "Covenant Marriage," *Ensign*, November 1996, 26.

7. Douglas Brinley, *Toward a Celestial Marriage* (Salt Lake City: Bookcraft, 1986), 7.

8. Kenneth W. Matheson, in *Living a Covenant Marriage*, ed. Douglas E. Brinley and Daniel K Judd (Salt Lake City: Deseret Book, 2004), 189.

9. Wendy L. Watson, *Let Your Spirit Take the Lead* (Salt Lake City: Deseret Book, 2004), audio CD.

CHAPTER THREE

FIVE SCRIPTURES THAT WILL IMPROVE YOUR FAMILY RELATIONSHIPS

᪐ Before we continue our discussion of marriage and family, let me share with you my credentials. I have none. You may close the book now if you wish (unless you're using my words as a sleeping aid). I have no training in marriage and family counseling. I do, however, have a love for the scriptures, and we both have the gift of the Holy Ghost, so perhaps together we can learn something. Now that we have the disclaimer out of the way, let's get to work.

Marriage is wonderful. Within a home created by two covenant-keeping adults, the Lord has an ideal place to send children. In such a place, all kinds of things can grow—love, happiness, joy, and children, not to mention stress, bills, and mortgages. Having children also *grows* marriage partners in a hundred ways. While it's true that

adults produce children, it's also true that children produce adults. For example, nothing will take the selfishness
out of a parent faster than a sick or injured child. When a
tiny one is hurting, all self-centered desires depart at warp
speed.

Children also *grow* their parents by giving them a
crash course in patience, kindness, empathy, sacrifice, toy
repair, and a dozen other virtues. Children teach us
humility by reminding us every day that we are much less
than perfect. These lessons are not easy. If most parents
had to evaluate their progress, I suspect they would say
that their children were *trying* their patience more than
growing it. Fortunately, we have help. By divine design, the
home is the perfect laboratory for learning and applying
gospel principles, and the scriptures are the perfect guide
for how to run the lab.

SCRIPTURE ONE:
"We lived after the manner of happiness" (2 Nephi 5:27)

Soon after arriving in the promised land, Nephi and
his followers separated from the Lamanites, built a temple,
and kept the commandments. Nephi describes this condition as living "after the manner of happiness."

Someone once said that a puritan is someone who
lives in mortal fear that someone, somewhere, is enjoying
himself. Unfortunately, many of our young people think

the gospel is just a list of rules designed to make sure they don't have any fun. How sad! Saying the gospel is just a list of things you can't do is like saying that a library is just a place where you can't talk. The gospel is not just a list of do's and don'ts. It's a way of life—a way of living after the manner of happiness.

The chief judge Giddonah asked Korihor the antichrist, "Why do ye teach this people that there shall be no Christ, to *interrupt their rejoicings?*" (Alma 30:22; emphasis added). In other words, those of us who believe in Christ should be *continually* rejoicing! If our children can't see the joy that gospel living brings us, they may conclude that there's another way to live that will make them happier.

If the Lord had a mission statement, it might be Moses 1:39: "To bring to pass the immortality and eternal life of man." By contrast, Satan's mission statement, from 2 Nephi 2:27, might read: "To make all men miserable like unto himself." His is the plan of misery, for "wickedness never was happiness" (Alma 41:10). However, Satan is a liar, and he teaches that real happiness comes from doing whatever you want to do and in giving in to every desire.

When our children go off into the world, they will be told that gospel living is restrictive. They will hear things like, "Man, in your church you can't do anything." This is an old tactic. Korihor taught that those who believed in

Christ were "in bondage," "bound down," and "yoked" by believing such foolish things. He also questioned the motives of the religious leaders of the time. Using language that we often hear today, he concluded that the people were unable to "enjoy their rights and privileges" (Alma 30:27). Satan will always focus people on rights without mentioning responsibilities.

While attending Brigham Young University, I was intrigued to see ideas similar to Korihor's coming from a sports writer from a rival university. His article, addressed to the BYU student body, supposedly was about his school's chances in an upcoming athletic contest. But the majority of the article was about how Latter-day Saints are in bondage! He wrote:

> Just think of the character it takes to let your bishopric and triple combination make all your life's decisions for you. That way, you don't have to waste any time pondering those important life questions like whether or not you should get married, have kids or pierce your ears more than once.
>
> Divine revelation is there to do it for you. I'm being serious now when I say that I'm kind of jealous about the other myriad benefits of having all your decisions made for you. . . .

How nice it must be to have the Honor Code
right there to instruct you in some manners.[1]

Make no mistake about it; someone this articulate and
this sarcastic will approach our children some day. That
confrontation will probably come when our children are
at school, and when we, their parents, are at home or
work. The response our children give in that pivotal
moment will come from the training they received at
home. They had better know by experience and by
example that choosing to live the gospel and choosing
obedience to the gospel is truly "living after the manner of
happiness."

What can we do to prepare them for that event? We
can show them the joy that living the gospel brings. I've
learned from personal experience that it's easy for my
children to see my frustration, my impatience, and my
stress, but I have to make a conscious and deliberate effort
to let them see the joy that comes from striving to live
what I know to be true.

What else can we do? On Sundays, we can be sure
that we never complain about how far we have to drive or
how early the new meeting schedule is or how hard the
benches are. We can show our children that scripture
study is about discovery, not drudgery, and that family
home evening is a time to laugh as well as learn. We can

let our children hear the excitement in our voices as we discuss a new insight we learned in gospel doctrine class. We can bear our testimony at Church and in more subtle ways at home.

We can teach our children at an early age the joy of doing something for someone else. We can plan family service projects or leave gifts at the neighbor's door, thus letting our children feel the secret happiness of anonymous giving. The main example of gospel living our children see is us. We want them to see our obedience, but we also want them to see our joy.

Perhaps more important than what our children see, however, is what they experience. By doing the little things mentioned above, we create the opportunity for spiritual experiences in the home. Research suggests that private religious behavior is the main predictor for the continued activity of our children later in life.[2]

In his remarkable address, King Benjamin expounded on benefits that come both in mortality and after death from living "after the manner of happiness."

> I would desire that ye should consider on the blessed and happy state of those that keep the commandments of God. For behold, they are blessed in all things, both temporal and spiritual; and if they hold out faithful to the

end they are received into heaven, that thereby they may dwell with God in a state of never-ending happiness. O remember, remember that these things are true; for the Lord God hath spoken it. (Mosiah 2:41)

Scripture One motivates us to show our children that we *love* being Latter-day Saints. We want them to know that our membership in the Church is not a pressure but a privilege. We want them to know the freedom—not the bondage—that comes from keeping the commandments of God. We want them to experience the presence of the Spirit in our homes. We want them to know that happiness in life isn't an accident. Lehi taught plainly that "if there be no righteousness there be no happiness" (2 Nephi 2:13).

Thus, happiness comes from following the path that leads to happiness. Or, as the Prophet Joseph Smith taught, "Happiness is the object and design of our existence; and will be the end thereof, if we pursue the path that leads to it; and this path is virtue, uprightness, faithfulness, holiness, and keeping all the commandments of God."[3] That is the perfect description of living "after the manner of happiness."

SCRIPTURE TWO:
*"Thou shalt teach them diligently unto thy children,
and shalt talk of them when thou sittest in thine house,
and when thou walkest by the way, and when thou liest down,
and when thou risest up"* (Deuteronomy 6:7)

I love this scripture (and not just because it contains the phrase "by the way"). This verse reminds me that whatever else I do as a parent, I am always a teacher. From the moment I rise up until the moment I lie down, I am teaching my children. My wife and I daily model what parents do, so among the other things my children learn from us is how to be moms and dads. Hence, in a very real way, when I teach my children, I am also teaching my grandchildren.

I am the father of four children five years old and under. What a party! Our home is in a constant state of chaos, which keeps me on my toes. I only wish the children would stay this young forever because most of their problems are small and easily solved.

I am absolutely amazed at the number of opportunities I have every day to teach my children. Whenever I walk up the stairs with a toddler in tow, I count the stairs out loud. Now my children count with me. Whenever I'm working in the house or in the yard, I tell them in detail what I'm doing, and usually they listen.

One day, while running an errand in the minivan, I

realized I had another opportunity to teach. My kids were strapped into their seatbelts and weren't going anywhere, so I turned off the talk-radio show and started singing the alphabet song. (When I'm driving and my kids are in the car, Mr. Limbaugh, Mr. Hannity, and Dr. Laura just have to survive without me.)

I suspect that our greatest teaching will not be in what we say but in what we are. My father joined the Church at age twenty-four and became a devoted student of the gospel. He was a geologist by trade, but he always took his "Church briefcase" with him to work. Within his briefcase were his high-priest-sized scriptures, a notepad, a red pencil, and a commentary or two. One day my mother explained that Dad left the house early so he could study the scriptures for half an hour before work. I knew Dad loved the scriptures, not because he told me he did but because I witnessed it myself.

Dad, as well as Mom, also loved good music, and it was constantly playing in my home. Many missionaries discover the Mormon Tabernacle Choir while on their missions as they replace old music-listening habits with new ones. Not me. Listening to the Tab Choir on my mission usually made me homesick. Every Sunday morning, Dad would be up early preparing a lesson while listening to the choir. We didn't need alarm clocks in our house on

Sunday mornings; we had Alexander Schreiner and Jerold Ottley.

Later, when I returned home from a mission and enrolled in a music appreciation class at the University of Utah, I already knew most of the classical music the teacher was playing. I think I embarrassed myself when I said a little too loudly, "Hey, that's the *Moldau*. I've heard that before." A good spirit accompanies good music, and that is part of what my parents taught me.

Scripture Two suggests that parents teach "when thou sittest in thine house," making our homes the most important classroom our children attend, particularly when it comes to spiritual things. The LDS Bible Dictionary defines the temple as follows: "A place where the Lord may come, it is the most holy of any place of worship on the earth. Only the home can compare with the temple in sacredness."[4]

Imagine pulling a TV and VCR into the chapel and showing a tape of the sitcom *Friends*. Imagine how we would grimace at the sexual innuendos. Imagine how we would wince at the Lord's name being taken in vain. We would consider it terribly inappropriate to watch a show like that in the chapel. But the definition we just read from the Bible Dictionary states that the home is a more sacred place than the stake center, the multipurpose room, or the chapel. In fact, the only place that can compare to the sacredness of the home is the temple. I don't even want to think about viewing a sitcom like *Friends* in the temple. The idea alone makes my skin crawl.

One of the things that helped bring my father into the Church was the feeling he had when he entered my mother's home on their first date. Her home felt different from anything he'd experienced before. It felt like a temple.

When it comes to testimony, and just about everything else, perhaps actions speak louder than words. My father never came to my bed at night and said, "I would indeed by ungrateful if I didn't stand on my feet this day and bear my testimony to you." He was a man of few words, but there was testimony in his actions. I watched him bear his witness every day when he left for work with his Church briefcase. I knew my Dad knew. And that helped me when I wasn't sure if I knew. Elder Jeffrey R. Holland spoke of the importance of parents letting their children know that they know:

> Parents simply cannot flirt with skepticism or cynicism, then be surprised when their children expand that flirtation into full-blown romance. If in matters of faith and belief children are at risk of being swept downstream by this intellectual current or that cultural rapid,

we as their parents must be more certain than ever to hold to anchored, unmistakable moorings clearly recognizable to those of our own household. It won't help anyone if we go over the edge with them, explaining through the roar of the falls all the way down that we really did know the Church was true and that the keys of the priesthood really were lodged there but we just didn't want to stifle anyone's freedom to think otherwise. No, we can hardly expect the children to get to shore safely if the parents don't seem to know where to anchor their own boat. . . .

I think some parents may not understand that even when they feel secure in their own minds regarding matters of personal testimony, they can nevertheless make that faith too difficult for their children to detect. We can be reasonably active, meeting-going Latter-day Saints, but if we do not live lives of gospel integrity and convey to our children powerful heartfelt convictions regarding the truthfulness of the Restoration and the divine guidance of the Church from the First Vision to this very hour, then those children may, to our regret but not surprise, turn out *not* to be visibly

active, meeting-going Latter-day Saints or
sometimes anything close to it.[5]

I am grateful that my parents tried to have family
home evening. At times it worked fairly well, and at other
times it didn't work at all. But they tried. Somehow, however, I learned the doctrines of the gospel anyway. I suspect that most of what I learned was probably taught in
the hundreds of teaching moments between the Monday
nights.

When I attended Primary, we sang songs about trees
whose blossoms resembled popcorn and about small spi-
ders ascending rain gutters. Today I am delighted to see
my children learning doctrine in Primary! They sing
songs like "Search, Ponder, and Pray" and "Follow the
Prophet."[6] Members of the Church have probably noticed
an increased sense of urgency to teach children the basic
doctrines of the gospel. This sense of urgency is perhaps
even more important at home. Elder Henry B. Eyring has
taught:

> The best time to teach is early, while chil-
> dren are still immune to the temptations of
> their mortal enemy, and long before the words
> of truth may be harder for them to hear in the
> noise of their personal struggles.
>
> A wise parent would never miss a chance

to gather children together to learn of the doctrine of Jesus Christ. Such moments are so rare
in comparison with the efforts of the enemy.
For every hour the power of doctrine is introduced into a child's life, there may be hundreds
of hours of messages and images denying or
ignoring the saving truths.

The question should not be whether we
are too tired to prepare to teach doctrine or
whether it wouldn't be better to draw a child
closer by just having fun or whether the child
isn't beginning to think that we preach too
much. The question must be, "With so little
time and so few opportunities, what words of
doctrine from me will fortify them against the
attacks on their faith which are sure to come?"
The words you speak today may be the ones
they remember. And today will soon be gone.[7]

The Doctrine and Covenants provides Latter-day parents with a "Things to Teach" list, and it mentions a sobering consequence if we fail to share the curriculum:

And again, inasmuch as parents have children in Zion, or in any of her stakes which are
organized, that teach them not to understand
the doctrine of repentance, faith in Christ the

Son of the living God, and of baptism and the gift of the Holy Ghost by the laying on of the hands, when eight years old, the sin be upon the heads of the parents. (D&C 68:25)

I love being a parent, and I feel a tremendous motivation for teaching my children the gospel. When Alma the Elder challenged those about to be baptized "to stand as witnesses of God at all times and in all things, and in all places" (Mosiah 18:9), he must have meant parents too. Therefore, I need to stand as a witness for my children and teach them at *all* times—including when I'm sitting in my house, when I'm walking by the way, when I'm lying down, and when I'm getting up.

SCRIPTURE THREE:
"This is my beloved Son, in whom I am well pleased"
(Matthew 3:17)

Scripture Three, familiar to Latter-day Saints, describes an event from the baptism of Jesus. What does the baptism of Jesus have to do with strengthening family relationships? Good question. Let's take a closer look at what's happening in this verse. This is a *father* talking about his *son* in the presence of many people. Notice the words the Father spoke. He didn't just say, "This is my son." He said, "This is my *beloved* son." In other words, "I love him." And it doesn't end there; the verse continues: "in whom I am well pleased." That is to say, "I'm proud of him; I'm pleased with his work."

We're all trying to become like our Father in Heaven, and here he is talking about his son in terms of love and praise. Doesn't this scripture give us a model of how we should talk about our own children in the presence of others? (We seldom hear the Father's voice in the scriptures, which makes this verse even more precious. Similar language can be found in Matthew 17:5, 3 Nephi 11:7, Joseph Smith–History 1:17, and 2 Peter 1:17.)

We're living in a time when put-downs outnumber build-ups, and although clever insults generate applause on sitcoms, they are hurtful and damaging within families. Home is the one place that every family member ought to feel completely safe. King Benjamin taught that when parents allow ridicule and unkind teasing among siblings, they are allowing their children to serve the adversary:

> And ye will not suffer your children that they go hungry, or naked; neither will ye suffer that they transgress the laws of God, and fight and quarrel one with another, and serve the devil, who is the master of sin, or who is the evil spirit which hath been spoken of by our fathers, he being an enemy to all righteousness.

74

> But ye will teach them to walk in the ways of
> truth and soberness; ye will teach them to love
> one another, and to serve one another. (Mosiah
> 4:14–15)

When I was growing up, I often heard my parents observe, "You treat your friends better than you do your own family." Perhaps because there were so many of us in a small home, and perhaps because we knew each other's faults so well, we tended to treat each other with less respect than we should have. Now, as a parent, I can see that I am sometimes guilty of a similar mistake: I treat visitors to our home better than I treat my children. President Ezra Taft Benson taught:

> Praise your children more than you cor-
> rect them. Praise them for even their smallest
> achievement. Encourage your children to
> come to you for counsel with their problems
> and questions by listening to them every day.
> . . . Treat your children with respect and kind-
> ness—just as you would when guests are pre-
> sent. They are, after all, more meaningful to
> you than guests. Teach your children never to
> speak unkindly to others regarding members
> of the family. Be loyal to one another.[8]

A University of Iowa study revealed "that the average two-year-old receives 432 negatively oriented statements a day to 32 positive ones."[9] I can understand that completely. The word my two-year-old hears the most is probably "No!" But a fourteen-to-one ratio of negative to positive? I sure would like to even up those numbers a little bit.

Most of us have entertained kindly thoughts about others, but sometimes those thoughts don't make it out of our mouths and become words. Praise is one thing we shouldn't keep to ourselves. In fact, President Benson taught that withholding praise is a sign of pride. "[Pride] is manifest in so many ways, such as fault-finding, gossiping, backbiting, murmuring, living beyond our means, envying, coveting, *withholding gratitude and praise that might lift another,* and being unforgiving and jealous."[10] People aren't usually criticized into change, but they might be loved or praised into change.

The wonderful thing about lifting others is that we lift ourselves in the process. Elder Neal A. Maxwell suggested that one of the ways we can manage our own vexing feelings of inadequacy is to "add to each other's storehouse of self-esteem by giving deserved, specific commendation more often. We should remember, too, that those who are breathless from going the second mile need deserved praise just as the fallen need to be lifted up."[11]

Giving praise is not a difficult thing to do. There's no huge lifestyle change required here. Just speak the praise you think. Or you could put your praise in a note. One mother left a note for her fourteen-year-old daughter every day. The notes said things such as, "I love your sense of humor," "Thanks for helping me with the dog," and "I am so glad you were born." One day the mother went into her daughter's room looking for something. As she left the room, she discovered that her daughter had stuck fifty of her favorite notes on the back of her door. Whenever she left her room, she was greeted with notes of praise from her mother.[12] This mother's spoken praise became more permanent because it was in print.

How long does it take to write a few encouraging words on a sticky note? A few seconds at the most. Is it expensive? No. Could it strengthen your family? Certainly. You could even paraphrase Scripture Three on a note: "I love you, son, and I'm so pleased with all you do."

I've yet to meet a teenager who isn't hungry to receive praise from his parents. I know that I relished any words of commendation I received from my father when I was young and insecure. Researchers Brent L. Top and Bruce A. Chadwick have written:

> Parents probably praise their teenagers
> more than their children give them credit for,

but all parents find themselves at times being overcritical with teens. Many of the young people [in our research] saw their mistakes as learning experiences and wanted to put them behind them, but their parents continued to rehash them. Generous praise helps young people to develop the self-esteem or self-confidence that will help them through the difficult teen years and to confidently assume adult roles. It can be discouraging for anyone, but especially teens who naturally struggle with feelings of inadequacy, to feel as if nothing they do is ever good enough. In contrast to continual criticism and an absence of praise, expressions of acceptance are actually motivational. Children who feel praised and recognized for their efforts as well as their deeds try harder to do even better.[13]

I never want my children to say, "I wonder what it would have been like to hear my Dad say nice things about me." Instead, I want them to know that I'm one of their biggest fans, and I can do something about that tonight.

Scripture Three is a gem. It's a concise model of how we can talk *to* and *about* our children in the presence of others. The Father's words were directed to those who witnessed the baptism of Jesus, but I've often wondered what it must have done for the Savior himself to hear these words of praise from the Father.

SCRIPTURE FOUR:
"Thou art still chosen" (D&C 3:10)

The prophet Joseph Smith received the revelation contained in the third section of the Doctrine and Covenants after Martin Harris had lost the 116-page manuscript. In the middle of a reprimand, the Lord assured Joseph that he was still in favorable standing: "But remember, God is merciful; therefore, repent of that which thou hast done which is contrary to the commandment which I gave you, and thou art still chosen, and art again called to the work" (D&C 3:10).

You may recall that Joseph suffered severe mental anguish at the loss of the manuscript. When he learned that Martin had let the manuscript out of his hands, he cried, "All is lost! All is lost! What shall I do? I have sinned—it is I who tempted the wrath of God. I should have been satisfied with the first answer which I received from the Lord; for he told me that it was not safe to let the writing go out of my possession." Joseph's mother reported, "He wept and groaned, and walked the floor continually."[14]

We can only imagine the hope and warmth that must have filled Joseph's heart when he heard the words, "Thou art still chosen." The fact is, Joseph was told a number of times that his sins were forgiven, and while it is true that the Lord cannot look upon sin with the least degree of allowance, it is also true that we worship a God who forgives.

The Son of God never made any mistakes, but the rest of God's children do. Our own children will also make mistakes, and the way we respond in these situations is critical. Certainly we would want our children to understand why what they did was wrong, and we hope that they will learn from their mistakes. But I suggest we can learn a great deal from the Lord's words to Joseph: "Thou art still chosen."

How do you praise people who haven't done anything praiseworthy? I once listened to a BYU Education Week presentation by Dr. James MacArthur, author of *Everyday Parents Raising Great Kids.* He showed parents how their praise is often given in one of two areas, or boxes: the "Do" box and the "Be" box.

BASED ON PERFORMANCE

BASED ON EXISTENCE

Dr. MacArthur suggested that most of the time, the praise we give our children is based on performance. If our children do something well, we praise them for what they did. This is appropriate and desirable. But Dr. MacArthur urged parents not to forget the "Be" box. We should also praise our children based on their worth as human beings, or as sons and daughters of God. The "Be" box is on the bottom—it's foundational.

I noticed a beautiful illustration of the "Do" and "Be" boxes while watching a rerun of my favorite TV program, *The Andy Griffith Show.* In this particular episode, Sheriff Andy Taylor's son, Opie, came home from school one day with a straight-A report card. Surprised and delighted, Opie's father showered him with praise, and Aunt Bee baked him his very own butterscotch pecan pie. Opie was also awarded a brand-new bicycle. All of this well-deserved recognition was given in the "Do" box, based on Opie's performance.

Later we learn that Opie's teacher had made a mistake—she had given him the wrong report card. Sheriff Taylor had boasted all over town about his son's academic achievements, and Opie felt terrible when he pondered the thought of telling his dad that he had actually flunked math and earned several C's.

Andy eventually learned about Opie's real report card and set off to find him and ask him why he hadn't

mentioned the mistake. But when Andy went up to his
son's room, he discovered a note from Opie saying that
he had run away from home. Andy finally found Opie
walking alone on a dirt road. Before Andy could say anything, however, Opie, always the honest kid, told his
father what had happened:

> Pa, there's somethin' you don't know, but
> you're gonna find out, so I might as well tell
> ya. I didn't get all A's on my report card. The
> teacher made a mistake. I wanted to tell you
> about it. I started to. But I knew you'd be awful
> disappointed. So I just never did. Then I got to
> thinkin' about it, and I figured the best thing to
> do would be to run away, and not come back
> 'til I was able to do somethin' to make you
> proud of me again.

At this point, Andy paused, took a deep breath, and
switched beautifully from the "Do" box to the "Be" box.
He stooped to the ground, looked up into Opie's eyes,
and said:

> Opie, I've got, I've got something I want
> to say to you. When I thought you got all A's,
> that was the most important thing in the world
> to me. And I made it so important that I made

it impossible for you to live up to. You're my
son. And I'm proud of you just for that. You do
the best you can, and if you do that, that's all
I'll ever ask of you.[15]

Opie was assured that he was valued based on the
mere fact that he was his father's son. That's the "Be" box.
That's praise based on existence. When I hear this story,
I imagine our Father in Heaven looking down on us and
saying, "You're my children. And I love you just for that.
Do the very best you can, and I'll send my Son to help
you when you make mistakes."

I believe the Lord uses both boxes. I'm encouraged
when I read about the calling of Moses and Enoch. Moses
responded to his call by telling the Lord that he was "of a
slow tongue" (Exodus 4:10). Enoch also said that he was
"slow of speech" and that all the people hated him (Moses
6:31). Moses and Enoch were judging their worth based
on performance. The Lord, however, looks on the heart,
and he assured them that he wasn't calling them based on
their public speaking ability but on something deeper that
only he could see.

The Lord will take us where we're at, and he'll work
with us. Some have taken the Lord's love and mercy too
far and have concluded, "The Lord loves me just the way
I am." While this is probably true, I also believe that the

Lord wants us to be something better. I don't believe he wants us to be content where we are. Rather, I think he often fills us with "divine discontent"[16] so that we'll keep striving, trying, and growing. Along the way, we'll make mistakes, but we can remember the reassuring words spoken to Joseph: "repent . . . and thou art still chosen."

Sometimes the chosen generation will choose the wrong. As a father, I always want my children to know they can come to me when they make a mistake or a poor choice. Elder H. Burke Peterson taught, "When children and teenagers are loved because of who they are and not for how they behave, only then can we begin to help make much-needed changes in behavior."[17]

Joseph Smith was responsible for the loss of an absolutely priceless manuscript, yet the Lord assured him that he was still chosen. Similarly, I want my children to know that they are "still chosen" even though they may make dumb mistakes or lose something much less consequential, such as their dad's palm pilot (we eventually found it).

SCRIPTURE FIVE:
"I began to be desirous that my family should partake of it also" (1 Nephi 8:12)

As soon as Lehi tasted the fruit of the tree of life, his thoughts (and his head) turned immediately toward his family. The fruit of the tree filled him with "exceedingly great joy," and Lehi wanted his family to taste as he had tasted. I love this verse because it demonstrates the love of a father toward his wife and children.

When something wonderful happens to you, who is the first person you want to share it with? Your answer reveals which relationships are most important to you. It's instructive that Lehi did not say, "I was desirous that my coworkers at the office should partake" or "I was desirous that the guys I play basketball with should partake." His first thoughts went out to his immediate family. We know that the family is the most important unit in time and eternity and that salvation is a family affair, so our *feelings* about family ought to be consistent with our *doctrine* about family.

They say that shared time plus shared experiences equals closeness. Perhaps the greatest protection we can give our children is to raise them in a close family. Growing close as a family is tougher than ever these days because the challenges of latter-day living seem determined to pull us apart.

I haven't set my alarm clock for a long time because I have a four-year-old little boy who seems to need no sleep. Early every morning he pounces on me and says, "Dad, can we play air hockey?" or "Dad, do you want to play pirate ship?" (Mom is fun to play pirate ship with too, but Dad makes better sound effects.) I dread that question. It hurts me to see the disappointment on his face when I answer every morning, "I'm sorry, Andrew, I have to go to work." It's like getting hit in the stomach.

One day as I was driving to the office I thought to myself, "Who came up with this arrangement? Why is it I have to break my son's heart every morning?" If I get home from work around 5:30 p.m., I have only about three hours with my family until bedtime. If children are so important, why don't I get to spend more time with mine? And while we're on the subject, how come I don't get to spend more time with my wife? Someone once joked that we're married for eternity but separated for life. (Sorry for the rant—I realize that we're all in the same boat.)

I finally decided to blame it all on the industrial revolution. If we were all farmers, maybe we could at least work together as families. My children spend more of each day away from me than with me. What a sobering and frightening thought—friends and school get more time with my kids than I do! Fortunately, I married well, and at least my children get to spend time with their wonderful mother. The stripling warriors in the Book of Mormon show us how important that can be.

Bottom line: I've learned that I have to fight for every minute I get with my family. I've learned to say "No" more often to things that take me away from my role as a husband and father.

"Quality time" is a phrase used in time-management seminars. My children don't have any idea what "quality time" means. Whether I say, "I don't have time for you right now" or "I don't have *quality* time for you right now" makes little difference to them. They just know that I'm going to be somewhere else. I've discovered that playing pirate ship or air hockey with my son is more satisfying than getting attention or applause from people I hardly know. I've learned that the old saying is right on: "No one on their deathbed is going to say they wish they had spent more time at the office." What Father Lehi taught me in Scripture Five is that I should thoughtfully and prayerfully identify the most joyous and wonderful things in life and then make sure my family partakes of them with me.

What are the fruits I want to share with my family? Certainly, the first one is the one Lehi tasted—the love of God manifested through the atonement of Christ. Lehi didn't say that it was "one of the best" he'd ever had; his description was much stronger than that. He called it "most sweet, above all that I ever before tasted" (1 Nephi 8:11). This particular fruit must be a daily minimum requirement in our family's spiritual diet. Partaking of the love of God allows us to enjoy everything else. Without it, no diet will sustain us through life's mists of darkness.

What other joys do I desire for my family? Here are a few I've found particularly tasty:

- The joy of discovering the scriptures
- The joy of service to others
- The joy of learning
- The joy of beautiful music
- The joy of nature
- The joy of family togetherness

Some of Satan's offerings are toxic, but he makes them appear desirable. Sometimes our children are unable to discern the difference between those things that will bring only short-term pleasure and those that will bring long-term joy. That's why it is so important that parents worthy of inspiration be standing at the tree of life. Part of my stewardship as a dad is to discern the best things for my family and to lead them to those things that will bring lasting joy. Without the leadership of righteous parents, our children may be tempted to try worldly enticements:

- The pleasure of mindless television
- The pleasure of non-stop video games
- The pleasure of pop culture
- The pleasure of fashion
- The pleasure of substance abuse
- The pleasure of immorality
- The pleasure of laziness
- The pleasure of materialism

These "pleasures" aren't fruits. They're more like Twinkies, or worse. Some of them are poison. None of these items were mentioned in Lehi's dream, probably because such things don't grow on trees that God has planted. They're only available in beat-up vending machines in the lobby of the great and spacious building. While much of the world consumes this stuff as if it were the only thing on the menu, we know that these things only satisfy temporarily and that no short-term fix can compare to long-term happiness.

Scripture Five teaches me that my goal as a father should be similar to Lehi's goal. Leave the dark and dreary wilderness behind, seek for life's greatest joys—the atonement of Christ being first and foremost—and lead my family to partake of them also.

CONCLUSION

The Lord sends us to earth in families. Families are that they might have joy, and the scriptures and the prophets testify that there is no lasting happiness outside the plan of happiness. Therefore, as the father of a young family, I am determined to live after the manner of happiness, to teach the gospel diligently to my children, to praise them in public and private, to let them know that they're "still chosen" when they make mistakes, and to be there at critical moments, always leading them to the fruit that is most joyous to the soul.

NOTES

1. Eric Walden, "The Great Debate: 'U' vs. 'Y,'" *The Daily Universe*, 21 November 2000, 6.

2. Brent L. Top and Bruce A. Chadwick, *Rearing Righteous Youth of Zion* (Salt Lake City: Bookcraft, 1998), 25–44.

3. Joseph Smith, *Teachings of the Prophet Joseph Smith*, sel. Joseph Fielding Smith (Salt Lake City: Deseret Book, 1976), 255–56.

4. Bible Dictionary, 781.

5. Jeffrey R. Holland, "A Prayer for the Children," *Ensign*, May 2003, 86.

6. *Children's Songbook* (Salt Lake City: The Church of Jesus Christ of Latter-day Saints, 1989), nos. 109 and 110.

7. Henry B. Eyring, "The Power of Teaching Doctrine," *Ensign*, May 1999, 73.

8. Ezra Taft Benson, *The Teachings of Ezra Taft Benson* (Salt Lake City: Bookcraft, 1988), 499.

9. Jack Canfield and Mark Victor Hansen, *Dare to Win* (New York: Berkley Book, 1994), 109–10.

10. Ezra Taft Benson, "Beware of Pride," *Ensign*, May 1989, 5; emphasis added.

11. Neal A. Maxwell, *Notwithstanding My Weakness* (Salt Lake City: Deseret Book, 1981), 10.

12. Canfield and Hansen, *Dare to Win*, 85–86.

13. Top and Chadwick, *Rearing Righteous Youth of Zion*, 110.

14. Lucy Mack Smith, *History of Joseph Smith by His Mother, Lucy Mack Smith* (Salt Lake City: Bookcraft, 1958), 128.

15. "Opie's Ill-Gotten Gain," *The Andy Griffith Show*, first aired 18 November 1963.

16. Neal A. Maxwell, "Becoming a Disciple," *Ensign*, June 1996, 18.

17. H. Burke Peterson, "Preparing the Heart," *Ensign*, May 1990, 83.

CHAPTER FOUR

FIVE SCRIPTURES THAT WILL STRENGTHEN YOUR FAITH

Everyone would like to have stronger faith. By themselves, the scriptures may not strengthen your faith, but being faithful to what they teach, does. In other words, faith cannot be separated from faithfulness. It's nice to know what to do, but faith comes in doing what you know. Elder Bruce R. McConkie taught:

> "Faith is a gift of God bestowed as a reward for personal righteousness. It is always given when righteousness is present, and the greater the measure of obedience to God's laws the greater will be the endowment of faith."[1]

A faithful person is rewarded with greater faith. We know from the fourth article of faith that faith is the first principle of the gospel. But we're not just talking about any kind of faith, we're talking about "faith *in the Lord Jesus Christ.*" This specialized type of faith is more powerful than lesser kinds of faith, such as self-confidence or a general positive attitude, because faith in Christ is connected to divine power.

SCRIPTURE ONE:
"How is it done? . . . Because of thy faith in Christ"
(Enos 1:7–8)

Enos wrote only one chapter in the Book of Mormon, but his message is vital. Enos began, "I will tell you of the wrestle which I had before God, before I received a remission of my sins" (Enos 1:2). Because all of us must receive a remission of our sins, Enos chose to write about something important to all of us. It's as if Enos were saying, "This *must* happen in your life. Here's how it happened in mine."

Initially, Enos went to hunt beasts in the forest, but he later began to reflect on the words his father had taught him. As they "sunk deep into [his] heart," he apparently lost all interest in hunting. He began to pray and continued praying all day and into the night, until finally a voice declared, "Enos, thy sins are forgiven thee, and thou shalt be blessed." Enos responded in gratitude and amazement: "Lord, how is it done?" The answer came,

"Because of *thy faith in Christ*" (Enos 1:3–7; emphasis added).

I like this scripture because of how easily we can apply the question "How is it done?" to our own lives. It really doesn't matter what "it" is; the formula is always the same—faith in Christ.

So what is the "it" you need to do? Cleanse your soul? (Enos 1:6). Build a ship? (1 Nephi 17:51). Defeat an army? (Alma 44:3–4). Conquer a habit? (Ether 12:27). Move a mountain? (Ether 12:30). Part a sea? (Exodus 14:13–16). Dismiss a demon? (Moses 1:21). Walk on water? (Matthew 14:29). Heal a relationship? (Alma 15:5–11). Resist a temptation? (Genesis 39:9–12). Level a prison? (Alma 14:27–28). For these many different challenges, there is but one single answer: faith in Christ. No matter what "it" is, the way "it" is accomplished is through the first principle of the gospel. (Read the verses above, and you'll be impressed with how they refer to faith in Christ.)

Jesus performed many miracles during his ministry. Today various Bible scholars (Bible *scholars* are not necessarily Bible *believers*) have discounted his miracles and reduced the Son of God to nothing but a great moral teacher. However, a moral teacher does not have the power to save, and miracles were evidence of the Savior's power to save. Clearly, Jesus performed miracles out of his love and compassion for others, but there was another important purpose in the things he did. Brother Robert J. Matthews has written:

> Jesus' miracles are a major part of his ministry. Without miracles the gospel has no saving power and is simply a philosophy. Without miracles there is no salvation, because man is fallen, unable to save himself, and must be rescued or redeemed by some person having greater power than mankind naturally has.[2]

From the Bible and the Book of Mormon, we learn that Jesus had power over everything—men and women, sickness, weather, animals, chemical elements, gravity, evil spirits, sin, plants, and death itself. Thus, Jesus had power over everything in the physical world. The message conveyed through his miracles is that if Jesus has such total power, we can have total faith in him.

Still, some were skeptical. They witnessed the Savior's power over tangible, visible things, such as healing a body, but they weren't so sure about his power over invisible things, like forgiving sins or healing the spirit. Notice the exact words Jesus used in this miraculous healing incident to answer that objection:

> And, behold, they brought to him a man sick of the palsy, lying on a bed: and Jesus seeing

their faith said unto the sick of the palsy; Son, be of good cheer; thy sins be forgiven thee. And, behold, certain of the scribes said within themselves, This man blasphemeth. And Jesus knowing their thoughts said, Wherefore think ye evil in your hearts? For whether is easier, to say, Thy sins be forgiven thee; or to say, Arise, and walk? *But that ye may know that the Son of man hath power on earth to forgive sins*, (then saith he to the sick of the palsy,) Arise, take up thy bed, and go unto thine house. (Matthew 9:2–6; emphasis added)

The message is that if Jesus can heal the visible body, he can also heal the invisible spirit. We can exercise complete and total faith in him because he has complete and total power over all things. Jesus' miracles are irrefutable evidence of what he declared to the apostles: "All power is given unto me in heaven and in earth" (Matthew 28:18).

When we exercise strong faith in Christ, we tap into his power to help us persevere through our afflictions. Without this kind of faith, our afflictions may bog us down and cause us to doubt. Elder Vaughn J. Featherstone has taught:

Number one on our agenda, above all else, is faith in Christ. I don't know anything that will take the place of it. Whenever we find problems in the Church, we usually find them under one of two umbrellas or canopies, either transgression or lack of faith in Christ.[3]

A note of caution: Faith is not willing our own desires into existence. That would be exercising faith in what *we* want. For example, many of us have experienced the death of a loved one and have concluded that if we'd only had more faith, the loved one could have been healed. But again, that is faith in what *we* want to happen, not faith in Christ and what he, in his wisdom, wants or allows to happen.

Jesus taught, "And again, it shall come to pass that he that hath faith in me to be healed, *and is not appointed unto death*, shall be healed" (D&C 42:48; emphasis added). When our faith in Christ is strong, we can be assured that "all things have been done in the wisdom of him who knoweth all things" (2 Nephi 2:24). This kind of faith allows us to pray with a measure of peace, acknowledging, "Not my will, but thine, be done" (Luke 22:42).

As we all know, even when our faith in Christ is strong, we still have problems. Jacob the brother of Nephi told the people that if they would pray with exceeding faith, God would "console [them] in [their] afflictions" (Jacob 3:1). Jacob didn't say that God would remove their afflictions but that he would comfort them and help them through. But even in our afflictions, if we can keep the faith and maintain the perspective the gospel offers, we'll be able to stay positive. Elder M. Russell Ballard has taught:

> The best thing about living a Christ-centered life, however, is how it makes you feel—inside. It's hard to have a negative attitude about things if and when your life is focused on the Prince of Peace. There will still be problems. Everyone has them. But *faith in the Lord Jesus Christ is a power to be reckoned with in the universe and in individual lives.* It can be a causative force through which miracles are wrought. It can also be a source of inner strength through which we find self-esteem, peace of mind, contentment, and the courage to cope. I have seen marriages saved, families strengthened, tragedies overcome, careers energized, and the will to go on living rekindled as people humble themselves before the Lord and accept His will in their lives. Heartache, tragedy, and trauma of all kinds can be focused and managed when the principles of the gospel of Jesus Christ are understood and applied.[4]

It's hard to have a negative attitude about *anything* when you have faith in the Lord Jesus Christ. Because of him, we know who we are. We know why we're here. We have taken upon us his name, and we belong to him (Mosiah 26:18). And it doesn't matter what "it" is; we'll get through "it." And how is "it" done? Because of our faith in Christ.

SCRIPTURE TWO:
"They that be with us, are more than they that be with them"
(2 Kings 6:16)

Everyone loves the Old Testament story of Elisha the prophet and his young servant. The attacking king of Syria had "compassed the city" with both horses and chariots, surrounding Elisha and his servant. After surveying their awful situation, the servant exclaimed, "Alas, my master! how shall we do?" Elisha responded, "Fear not: for they that be with us, are more than they that be with them" (2 Kings 6:14–16).

We can only imagine the servant counting in his head: "Let's see, there's two of us, and we're up against an entire army, and Elisha says we have more guys on our side than they have on theirs. I must be missing something." Elisha then prayed, saying, "Lord, I pray thee, open his eyes, that he may see." When the Lord opened the eyes of the young servant, he finally saw what Elisha saw: "the mountain was full of horses and chariots of fire round about Elisha" (2 Kings 6:17).

The gist of the story is this: As children of God, we are *not* alone, we never *were* alone, and we never *will be* alone. What was true then is true today: "They that be with us are more than they that be with them." When you've got God on your side, you cannot possibly be outnumbered because God and one other person is a majority. Paul assured the Romans, "If God be for us, who can be against us?" (Romans 8:31).

In the premortal existence, we stood with the two-thirds of the hosts of heaven who chose to follow the Father's plan. In the single most critical choice to be made in our first estate, we chose correctly and have now been sent to our second estate to make the choice again. Will we once again choose the Father's plan of happiness, or will we choose what we once rejected—Satan's plan of misery? This decision has got to be the ultimate no-brainer.

Now that we're on earth, God has not left us alone. If you've ever sung the hymn "How Firm a Foundation," you will recognize in the lyrics the Lord's promise to stay with us as recorded in Isaiah 41:10: "Fear thou not; for I am with thee: be not dismayed; for I am thy God: I will strengthen thee; yea, I will help thee; yea, I will uphold thee with the right hand of my righteousness." President

George Q. Cannon taught that because of our baptismal covenant, God would always be with us:

> When we went forth into the waters of baptism and covenanted with our Father in heaven to serve Him and keep His commandments, He bound Himself also by covenant to us that He would never desert us, never leave us to ourselves, never forget us, that in the midst of trials and hardships, when everything was arrayed against us, He would be near unto us and would sustain us.[5]

Thus we know that God is on our side, as are his angels. The Lord promised, "I will go before your face. I will be on your right hand and on your left, and my Spirit shall be in your hearts, and mine angels round about you, to bear you up" (D&C 84:88).

President John Taylor taught, "God lives, and his eyes are over us, and his angels are round and about us, and they are more interested in us than we are in ourselves, ten thousand times, but we do not know it."[6]

We have unseen friends on the other side of the veil who are intensely interested in our success. President Ezra Taft Benson testified:

> "If we only knew it, heavenly hosts are pulling for us—friends in heaven that we cannot

now remember who yearn for our victory. This is our day to show what we can do—what life and sacrifice we can daily, hourly, instantly make for God. If we give our all, we will get His all from the greatest of all.[7]

I was among several faculty members invited to speak to a large gathering of teenagers in the Denver, Colorado, area one August morning. I recall that more than three thousand gathered at a large convention center. At the beginning of the conference, a wonderful stake president opened the meeting and introduced a young woman on the front row. As she stood up and turned around to face thousands of her peers, all the lights in the large meeting room went dark except for one tiny spotlight directly over her head. She was the only person anyone could see in the whole room! The stake president announced that this young woman would be the only member of the Church in her entire high school when she began attending the following month.

Suddenly from the darkness, the young people in the convention center began to applaud. When the lights came back on, three thousand teenagers were on their feet, shouting cheers of encouragement and support for this young woman. I think what happened to her that day had more of an impact than anything any of the speakers said. She knew she was surrounded with support, and that knowledge would bless her every day of her first year of high school. She would be a light in the darkness, but she would not be alone.

Like this young woman, we cannot see much of the support available to us. *God* is on our side, the *Holy Ghost* is our companion, *angels* are round about us to bear us up, and *heavenly hosts* are pulling for our victory. Some of our support we can see, such as our fellow members of the Church around the world. More than eleven million Saints are with us in our desire to choose the right. Truly, "they that be with us are more than they that be with them."

Like Elisha's servant, we are missing something if we think we're alone. "Truth is knowledge of things as they are, and as they were, and as they are to come" (D&C 93:24), and when the Lord opens your eyes to the truth, you begin to see that you never *are* alone, you never *were* alone, and you never *will be* alone. That knowledge, if you cling to it, will fill you with faith every day for the rest of your life.

SCRIPTURE THREE:
"Fear not" (D&C 6:33–37)

It seems that whenever heavenly messengers come to earth, they always begin with the same words: "Fear not." It's like they're saying, "Why are you people so afraid all the time? Where's your faith? Fear not!" Sometimes the phrase "fear not" is repeated more than once. Scripture Three is one of those cases:

> *Fear not* to do good, my sons, for what-soever ye sow, that shall ye also reap; therefore, if ye sow good ye shall also reap good for your reward. Therefore, *fear not*, little flock; do good; let earth and hell combine against you, for if ye are built upon my rock, they cannot prevail. Behold, I do not condemn you; go your ways and sin no more; perform with soberness the work which I have commanded you. Look unto me in every thought; doubt not, *fear not*. Behold the wounds which pierced my side, and also the prints of the nails in my hands and feet; be faithful, keep my commandments, and ye shall inherit the kingdom of heaven. Amen. (D&C 6:33–37; emphasis added)

Isn't that a wonderful scripture? Fear is the opposite of faith, and you can't have both at the same time. The prophet Joseph Smith taught:

> Where doubt and uncertainty are there faith is not, nor can it be. For doubt and faith

do not exist in the same person at the same time; so that persons whose minds are under doubts and fears cannot have unshaken confidence; and where unshaken confidence is not there faith is weak.[8]

Simply stated, if we're going to keep the faith, we've got to lose the fear. One of the last things Jesus said to the apostles before he was betrayed was about fear: "Peace I leave with you, my peace I give unto you: not as the world giveth, give I unto you. Let not your heart be troubled, neither let it be afraid" (John 14:27). Elder Jeffrey R. Holland referred to the counsel to not let our hearts be troubled or afraid as a commandment, adding something that has become one of my favorite quotes of all time:

I submit to you, that [John 14:27] may be one of the Savior's commandments that is, *even in the hearts of otherwise faithful Latter-day Saints,* almost universally disobeyed; and yet I wonder whether our resistance to this invitation could be any more grievous to the Lord's merciful heart. I can tell you this as a parent: as concerned as I would be if somewhere in their lives one my children were seriously troubled or unhappy or disobedient, nevertheless I

would be infinitely more devastated if I felt
that at such a time that child could not trust
me to help or thought his or her interest was
unimportant to me or unsafe in my care. In
that same spirit, I am convinced that none of
us can appreciate how deeply it wounds the
loving heart of the Savior of the world when
He finds that His people do not feel confident
in His care or secure in His hands or trust in
His commandments.[9]

I had never considered this idea before. We may actually hurt the Savior's feelings if we do not come to him
when we're troubled or afraid. Before I heard Elder
Holland's talk, I had never thought of the phrase "Let not
your heart be troubled" as a commandment, but I do now.
Since Jesus overcame the world, he is the perfect being to
go to when we're overcome with fear.

The news headlines during the past few years induce
more fear than any I've ever read. I've often wondered
how the First Presidency and the Quorum of the Twelve
react when they read the morning news. Perhaps you've
wondered too, but we don't have to wonder for long.
Every six months they tell us exactly what they think.
President Boyd K. Packer's talk called "Do Not Fear" in
the April 2004 general conference was precisely what I

needed to help me keep the faith and lose the fear.[10] On
an earlier occasion, President Packer talked specifically
about the kinds of reactions that leaders of the Church
have toward world events:

> This is a great time to live. When times
> are unsettled, when the dangers persist, the
> Lord pours out His blessings upon His church
> and kingdom. I have been associated now in
> the councils of the Church for upwards of
> thirty years. During that time I have seen,
> from the sidelines at least, many a crisis.
> Among the leaders I have at times seen great
> disappointment, some concern, maybe some
> anxiety. One thing I have never seen is fear.
> Fear is the antithesis of faith. In this Church
> and in this kingdom there is faith. So let us
> look forward with an attitude of faith and
> hope.[11]

If those men, with their collective wisdom, insight,
and inspiration, are not afraid, then perhaps I can follow
their example and not let the chaos in the world weaken
my faith.

Jesus said, "Wherefore, be of good cheer, and *do not
fear*, for I the Lord am with you, and will stand by you; and
ye shall bear record of me, even Jesus Christ, that I am the

Son of the living God, that I was, that I am, and that I am to come" (D&C 68:6; emphasis added).

SCRIPTURE FOUR:
"Hearken and hear, O ye my people, saith the Lord and your God, ye whom I delight to bless with the greatest of all blessings" (D&C 41:1)

We often think of God as a stern, omnipotent being, concerned only with law, judgment, justice, and punishment. No doubt he is concerned with those things, but the scriptures tell us there's much more to our Father. Scripture Four tells us that he delights to bless! God is literally our Father, in the best sense of that word, and he greatly desires to give good things to his children. Jesus taught:

> What man is there of you, whom if his son ask bread, will he give him a stone? Or if he ask a fish, will he give him a serpent? If ye then, being evil, know how to give good gifts unto your children, how much more shall your Father which is in heaven give good things to them that ask him? (Matthew 7:9–11)

Our Father in Heaven is sometimes called the "giver of good gifts" because of the description expressed in Matthew 7:11. Often, the key to receiving worthy gifts is to ask for them. James wrote, "Ye have not, because ye ask not" (James 4:2). But what kinds of things should we ask for? That's a good question.

Sometimes I've wondered if the things I pray about are too trivial or too unimportant when compared with everything else going on in the world. At least I *used* to think that until I had my own children. Now I think differently. If something is important to my five-year-old, it's important to me, no matter what other problems are on my mind.

In the Book of Mormon, the poor among the Zoramites were laboring under the false impression that they could only pray a memorized prayer from atop the Rameumptom. Amulek taught them that not only could they pray wherever they happened to be but also that they could pray for just about anything they needed:

> Yea, cry unto him for mercy; for he is mighty to save. Yea, humble yourselves, and continue in prayer unto him. Cry unto him when ye are in your fields, yea, over all your flocks. Cry unto him in your houses, yea, over all your household, both morning, mid-day, and evening. Yea, cry unto him against the power of your enemies.
>
> Yea, cry unto him against the devil, who is an enemy to all righteousness. Cry unto him

over the crops of your fields, that ye may prosper in them. Cry over the flocks of your fields, that they may increase. But this is not all; ye must pour out your souls in your closets, and your secret places, and in your wilderness.

Yea, and when you do not cry unto the Lord, let your hearts be full, drawn out in prayer unto him continually for your welfare, and also for the welfare of those who are around you. (Alma 34:18–27)

How can we apply this scripture to our day? I suspect that most people reading this book do not have fields, crops, and flocks. But I'm fairly sure they have jobs, mortgages, and bills. I'll bet they also have challenges, trials, and problems. And if these things matter to them, they must also matter to their perfect Father in Heaven, who delights to bless. So, to paraphrase Amulek, cry unto him over your job, that you may prosper in it. Cry over your assets, that they may increase so you can provide for your loved ones, support the missionary fund, increase your fast offerings, and help the sick and afflicted (Jacob 2:19). Pray for all of these things because if they're important to you, they're important to God.

One of the most repeated phrases in the scriptures is,

"Ask and ye shall receive." Read the following five verses and see if they don't stir up feelings of faith in your heart.

> Ask, and it shall be given you; seek, and ye shall find; knock, and it shall be opened unto you: For every one that asketh receiveth; and he that seeketh findeth; and to him that knocketh it shall be opened. (Matthew 7:7–8)

> Therefore, ask, and ye shall receive; knock, and it shall be opened unto you; for he that asketh, receiveth; and unto him that knocketh, it shall be opened. (3 Nephi 27:29)

> Ask, and ye shall receive; knock, and it shall be opened unto you. Amen. (D&C 4:7)

> Behold, I say unto you, go forth as I have commanded you; repent of all your sins; ask and ye shall receive; knock and it shall be opened unto you. (D&C 49:26)

> Draw near unto me and I will draw near unto you; seek me diligently and ye shall find me; ask, and ye shall receive; knock, and it shall be opened unto you. Whatsoever ye ask the Father in my name it shall be given unto you, that is expedient for you. (D&C 88:63–64)

We all know there are some things we shouldn't ask for. No one would pray, "And bless us that after we rob the bank we can get home in safety." Jesus taught the Nephites, "And whatsoever ye shall ask the Father in my name, *which is right*, believing that ye shall receive, behold it shall be given unto you" (3 Nephi 18:20; D&C 88:65; emphasis added).

I believe we are justified, indeed we are commanded, to pray for help in bringing about our righteous desires. And we don't pray without hope. We pray with the knowledge that our Father knows how to give good gifts and delights to bless his children.

SCRIPTURE FIVE:
"All things are possible to him that believeth" (Mark 9:23)

When I was a college student, I read about a sister who came up with an interesting strategy to help her gain stronger faith in the Lord. She reprinted all of her favorite faith-giving scripture passages on a piece of paper, and whenever she started to feel doubts and fears creep in, she read all of the scriptures to herself. I liked the idea. I'd always been told there was a power in the scriptures well beyond the power of other books, and I decided to try it for myself.

Hidden in the back of my day planner, I made a page labeled "Hope." On my Hope page, I listed a number of

scriptural references, hymn lyrics, excerpts from my patriarchal blessing, and inspired quotations. If I ever needed a
lift during the day, I'd go to my Hope page and it would
bolster my faith. Here are a few excerpts from my list. Try
the experiment yourself. Read through these verses and
see if you don't feel an uplifting influence:

> Therefore I say unto you, What things
> soever ye desire, when ye pray, believe that ye
> receive them, and ye shall have them. (Mark
> 11:24)

> Behold, I say unto you that whoso
> believeth in Christ, doubting nothing, whatso-
> ever he shall ask the Father in the name of
> Christ it shall be granted him; and this prom-
> ise is unto all, even unto the ends of the earth.
> (Mormon 9:21)

> And after that he came men also were
> saved by faith in his name; and by faith, they
> become the sons of God. And as surely as
> Christ liveth he spake these words unto our
> fathers, saying: Whatsoever thing ye shall ask
> the Father in my name, which is good, in faith
> believing that ye shall receive, behold, it shall
> be done unto you. (Moroni 7:26)

All flesh is in mine hands; be still and know that I am God. (D&C 101:16)

Be thou humble; and the Lord thy God shall lead thee by the hand, and give thee answer to thy prayers. (D&C 112:10)

If any of you lack wisdom, let him ask of God, that giveth to all men liberally, and upbraideth not; and it shall be given him. (James 1:5)

Jesus said unto him, If thou canst believe, all things are possible to him that believeth. (Mark 9:23)

But Jesus beheld them, and said unto them, With men this is impossible; but with God all things are possible. (Matthew 19:26)

Therefore, dearly beloved brethren, let us cheerfully do all things that lie in our power; and then may we stand still, with the utmost assurance, to see the salvation of God, and for his arm to be revealed. (D&C 123:17)

Therefore, be ye as wise as serpents and yet without sin; and I will order all things for your good, as fast as ye are able to receive them. Amen. (D&C 111:11)

Be not afraid, only believe. (Mark 5:36)

Faith is an action word. Sometimes, like doubting Thomas, we are tempted to say, "I'll believe it when I see it." But "seeing is believing" is the philosophy of the world. Someone once remarked that atheists don't find God for the same reason that bank robbers don't find police officers. They don't want to see them. They work hard not to see them. But that doesn't mean they don't exist.

When it comes to spiritual things, the world's phrase is reversed to "believing is seeing." Seeing angels didn't help Laman and Lemuel much. They saw but didn't believe. On the other hand, those in the scriptures who had strong belief first often saw things that rewarded their faith. When the Brother of Jared saw the finger of the Lord, the Lord said, "Because of thy *faith*, thou hast *seen*" (Ether 3:9; emphasis added).

When a blind man approached Jesus, the Savior asked, "What wilt thou that I should do unto thee?" The man responded, "Lord, that I might receive my sight. And Jesus said unto him, Go thy way; thy faith hath made thee whole. And immediately he received his sight, and followed Jesus" (Mark 10:51–52). In a literal way, this man believed and then saw. Believing is seeing.

King Benjamin pleaded with his people to believe so that they could see the results their faith would produce in their lives:

> Believe in God; believe that he is, and that he created all things, both in heaven and in earth; believe that he has all wisdom, and all power, both in heaven and in earth; believe that man doth not comprehend all the things which the Lord can comprehend. (Mosiah 4:9)

King Benjamin continued by promising the people that if they would believe in God and remember his long-suffering toward them, "standing steadfastly in the faith," they would "grow in the knowledge of the glory of him that created [them], or in the knowledge of that which is just and true" (Mosiah 4:11–12). In other words, what began as belief would grow into knowledge—believing would become seeing.

I often feel that I am ready, willing, and . . . well, two out of three ain't bad. Sometimes the best I can manage in life is to be willing. Every Sunday I promise that I am *willing* to take upon me the name of Jesus, that I am *willing* to always remember him, and that I am *willing* to keep his commandments, which he has given me. But I'm often not sure if I'm *able* to do everything I should. (You might say I need a cane 'cause I'm not able.)

However, I know in whom I have trusted! I am weak, but God is able. Nephi told his brothers, "The Lord is able to do all things according to his will, for the children of men, if it so be that they exercise faith in him" (1 Nephi 7:12). And that's the heart of it all—not faith in ourselves but faith in the Lord Jesus Christ. With that kind of faith, "all things are possible to him that believeth" (Mark 9:23).

CONCLUSION

Faith isn't like riding a bike—an ability we always have once we've learned it. Faith is more like growing a garden. You have to deliberately plant faith; then you've got to keep it watered and nurtured in order to help it grow. Those who strive to keep the faith soon discover that they've enlisted in the perpetual labor of pulling the weeds of doubt and fear that seem to grow spontaneously and thrive without any maintenance. I suppose there is opposition in all things, and that includes opposition in all gardens. However, there is help. The "Miracle Grow" for the plant of faith is contained in the standard works. Nothing seems to feed our faith like immersing ourselves in the scriptures. Paul taught, "Faith cometh by hearing, and hearing by the Word of God" (Romans 10:17).

How is it done? No matter what "it" is, we can do it because of our faith in Christ (Enos 1:7–8). So we fight on, knowing that "they that be with us are more than they that be with them" (2 Kings 6:16). We will "fear not" (D&C 6:33–37), knowing that God delights to bless his children (D&C 41:1). And we will doubt not because with God, all things are possible to those that believe (Mark 9:23).

NOTES

1. Bruce R. McConkie, *Mormon Doctrine,* 2d ed. (Salt Lake City: Bookcraft, 1979), 264.

2. Robert J. Matthews, *Behold the Messiah* (Salt Lake City: Bookcraft, 1994), 126.

3. Vaughn J. Featherstone, "The Torchbearer," *Brigham Young University 1982–83 Fireside and Devotional Speeches* (Provo, Utah: University Publications, 1983), 145.

4. M. Russell Ballard, *Our Search for Happiness* (Salt Lake City: Deseret Book, 1993), 15–16; emphasis added.

5. George Q. Cannon, *Gospel Truth: Discourses and Writings of George Q. Cannon,* sel. Jerreld L. Newquist, 2 vols. in 1 (Salt Lake City: Deseret Book, 1974), 134.

6. John Taylor, in *Journal of Discourses,* 26 vols. (London: Latter-day Saints' Book Depot, 1854–86), 23:221.

7. Ezra Taft Benson, "Jesus Christ—Gifts and Expectations," *Ensign,* December 1988, 6.

8. Joseph Smith, *Lectures on Faith* (Salt Lake City: Deseret Book, 1985), 6:12.

9. Jeffrey R. Holland, *Trusting Jesus* (Salt Lake City: Deseret Book, 2003), 68; emphasis added.

10. Boyd K. Packer, "Do Not Fear," *Ensign,* May 2004, 77–80.

11. Boyd K. Packer, *Things of the Soul* (Salt Lake City: Bookcraft, 1996), 195.

CHAPTER FIVE

FIVE SCRIPTURES
THAT WILL MOTIVATE YOU
TO ACTION

It could well be said of the scriptures, "Truer words were never spoken." That's why the scriptures have such power. We know they can be counted on. When we read a verse from the standard works, we don't have to ask, "Do you have a reference for that?" The scriptures *are* the reference. We don't have to ask, "Are you sure that's true?" We already *know* the scriptures are true. There's no need to scour footnotes or look for original sources because the scriptures come from the original source of the universe. Knowing the scriptures are true means we are obligated to be true to what we know.

Some people say scripture reading puts them to sleep; others say it wakes them up. The scriptures are not passive. They tell us to get up, get going, and get with it.

Following are five of my favorite scriptures that help me when I need a little motivation.

SCRIPTURE ONE:
"Awake, and arise from the dust" (Moroni 10:31)

Moroni's last words in the Book of Mormon are a wake-up call to "all the ends of the earth" (Moroni 10:24). His message is direct, clear, and unapologetic: Awake, come unto Christ, deny yourselves of all ungodliness, and I'll see you at the judgment bar (Moroni 10:31–34).

The scriptures often use sleep as a metaphor for being spiritually lazy. Isaiah urged Zion to "awake" and put on her "beautiful garments" (Isaiah 52:1). Lehi told his sons to "awake" and "put on the armor of righteousness" (2 Nephi 1:23). Nephi's younger brother Jacob told his brethren to "awake from the slumber of death" (Jacob 3:11). King Benjamin pleaded with his people to "awake to a remembrance of the awful situation of those that have fallen into transgression" (Mosiah 2:40). Alma invited the Zoramites to "awake and arouse [their] faculties" (Alma 32:27) as he taught them how to plant the testimony of Christ in their hearts. When God's children sin or simply do not live up to their spiritual potential, God sends prophets to shake them into spiritual consciousness.

Sometimes prophets have to use frightening images of chains and hell to roust us from our spiritual slumber.

Laman and Lemuel were physically present but in spiritual la-la land when Lehi tried to wake them up: "O that ye would awake; awake from a deep sleep, yea, even from the sleep of hell, and shake off the awful chains by which ye are bound. . . . Awake! and arise from the dust" (2 Nephi 1:13–14). (I don't know exactly what the "sleep of hell" is, but it's probably worse than a certain Boy Scout winter camp I'd like to forget.)

Sometimes our wake-up calls are less dramatic. Perhaps we've felt the Spirit at an inspiring fireside, been touched during general conference, or experienced a renewed desire to be a better person during our personal gospel study. This is our spiritual alarm clock saying, "Awake, and arise from the dust!"

The best thing that can happen when that alarm goes off is to get up and get with it. However, the spiritual alarm clock has a procrastination feature called the "snooze button" that is often a little too tempting: *I really want to start a scripture study program, but I'm going to wait until the kids are back in school. I know I need to stop wasting my time with television, and I will as soon as this season of reality shows is over.*

Sometimes even very good people can procrastinate the day of their awakening by making frequent use of the snooze button. Amulek was a decent man of "no small reputation," but his spiritual alarm clock rang for some time before he answered the call. He was ignoring his wake-up call, and he knew it: "I was called many times and I would not hear; therefore I knew concerning these things, yet I would not know" (Alma 10:4–6). The story of Amulek is particularly interesting because the Lord persisted with him, even though he had a pattern of repeatedly hitting the snooze button. That should give all of us hope even if we've continued in the same pattern.

Being awake has many advantages over being asleep, and being awake during the latter days is especially important. When we're awake, we hear the promptings of the Holy Ghost and can benefit from divine direction in every area of life. President Brigham Young observed:

> There is no doubt, if a person lives according to the revelations given to God's people, he may have the Spirit of the Lord to signify to him His will, and to guide and to direct him in the discharge of his duties, in his temporal as well as his spiritual exercises. I am satisfied, however, that in this respect, we live far beneath our privileges.[1]

Those who are spiritually asleep are living beneath their privileges. Brigham Young wasn't the only one to speak of what the Lord's people are missing out on when they're asleep on the job. Among the many concerns that must have caused distress to the Prophet Joseph Smith, Heber C. Kimball observed:

> The greatest torment he [Joseph Smith] had and the greatest mental suffering was because this people would not live up to their privileges. There were many things he desired to reveal that we have not learned yet, but he could not do it. He said sometimes that he felt pressed upon and as though he were pent up in an acorn shell, and all because the people did not and would not prepare themselves to receive the rich treasures of wisdom and knowledge that he had to impart.[2]

Along these same lines, I've often wondered what kind of messages we men of the Church could hear in general priesthood meeting if we didn't have to be reminded every six months to be decent husbands and fathers. What kind of spiritual treasures have we missed because we haven't awakened to our duty concerning the most simple and basic things?

Sometime when you have a minute, read the message Alma gave to the people of Zarahemla—people who were clearly living beneath their privileges—in Alma 5. Next, read the message he gave to the people of Gideon in Alma 7. Note the incredible difference in tone and content between the two addresses. Because those in Gideon were spiritually awake, they were privileged to hear some of the most powerful teachings in the scriptures about the Savior and the breadth of his atonement. (You may recall that Scripture Four from Chapter One of this book came from Alma's discourse in Gideon). Those in Zarahemla, on the other hand, had to be reminded once again of their duty.

Scripture One says, "Wake up!" In the words of Elder Sterling W. Sill, "You are to immediately stop doing all of the things that you . . . know that you should not do. . . . You are to immediately start doing all of the things that you . . . know that you should do."[3] Easier said than done? Of course it is, so start small. Stop doing the one thing that does the most to keep you from enjoying your spiritual privileges, and start doing the one thing that would bless your spiritual life the most. That's a great way to wake up.

Finally, keep your hands off that snooze button! Procrastination in spiritual matters is the sleep of hell spoken of by Father Lehi. Instead of snoozing, we can arise before it is "everlastingly too late" (Helaman 13:38) and "awake to a sense of [our] awful situation" (Ether 8:24).

Robert Louis Stevenson observed, "You cannot run away from a weakness. You must sometime fight it out or perish; and if that be so, *why not now*, and where you stand?"[4] What a powerful quotation. Yes, why not now? And if not now, when? When is a better time to wake up? Later? It's already later. It's the latter days for crying out loud. This is the worst time to be putting on the natural man (Mosiah 3:19). Scripture One says, "Wake up now. Procrastinate later."

The Japanese launched a surprise attack on Pearl Harbor in 1941. In the 1970 movie about that attack titled *Tora! Tora! Tora!* the character playing Adm. Isoroku Yamamoto, fully aware of the industrial might of the United States, made a grave and ultimately correct observation: "I fear all we have done is to awaken a sleeping giant and fill him with a terrible resolve." World War II has been over for more than fifty years, but Satan's war against righteousness rages on. Scripture One is like a spiritual alarm clock intended to awaken the sleeping giant, or the *spiritual* giant within each of us. Moroni's words can fill us with a wonderful resolve to come unto Christ, deny ourselves of all ungodliness, live up to our privileges, and prepare our families and the world for the Second Coming.

Elder Bruce R. McConkie once remarked that we are living in "the Saturday night of time and that on Sunday morning the Lord will come."[5] I suppose the Primary song is correct: "Saturday *is* a special day. It's the day we get ready for Sunday."[6] If the Lord is coming Sunday morning, there's no time to snooze. Scripture One is the Sunday morning alarm clock that says, "Up and at 'em, house of Israel; awake, and arise from the dust."

SCRIPTURE TWO:
"Ponder the path of thy feet" (Proverbs 4:26)

Now that we're awake, what do we do? Well, the first thing most people do when they get out of bed is put their feet on the floor. Feet have symbolic meaning in the scriptures. They represent how we choose to live, our personal direction, mission, or goals.[7] To ponder the path of our feet is to think about the purpose and direction of our life.

Suppose someone were to ask, "Why are you here?" We might answer, "Well, each of us came to earth to get a physical body, and we came to be tested to see if we would do whatsoever the Lord commanded us." Suppose the questioner interrupted us and said, "No, no, no, that's why *everybody* is here. Why are *you* here?" That's a different question. What is *your* life's mission? What will *you* give your life to? How will the world be a different place because you were here? When that question is asked, we begin to ponder the path of our feet. Where am I going? What am I working toward? What is at the end of this road?

Perhaps the greatest map for showing us which way to walk is found in the scriptures. The psalmist wrote, "Thy word is a lamp unto my feet, and a light unto my path" (Psalm 119:105). Thus, the scriptures light the way that we should walk by offering general direction for all of God's children.

Scriptural truths combined with the Holy Ghost offer a show-and-tell presentation as we ponder the path of our feet. Nephi taught that the "words of Christ will tell you all things what ye should do" (2 Nephi 32:3). While reading the scriptures, however, we may receive individualized revelation through the Spirit. Nephi continued, "If ye will enter in by the way, and receive the Holy Ghost, it will show unto you all things what ye should do" (2 Nephi 32:5). Note the words "show" and "tell." The scriptures tell, the Holy Ghost shows.

Latter-day Saints are greatly privileged to receive patriarchal blessings, which are usually more personal than the scriptures. President Ezra Taft Benson taught, "I would encourage you . . . to receive a patriarchal blessing. Study it carefully and regard it as personal scripture to you—for that indeed is what it is."⁸ A patriarchal blessing written for the benefit and blessing of one individual can be a lot more specific than the standard works, which were written for the benefit and blessing of billions. Sister Elaine Jack has taught:

> What does a patriarchal blessing say? Have you ever heard of one which says, "I am

sorry—you're a loser. Do the best you can on earth, and we'll see you in about seventy years." Of course not! And you never will, because of the divine qualities each of God's children has inherited. *A patriarchal blessing is like a road map, a guide, directing you in your walk through life.* It identifies your talents and the good things that can be yours.[9]

As you ponder the path of your feet in your walk through life, you may decide to compose a statement of your life's purpose. Most everyone is familiar with the idea of a mission statement. Organizations and individuals use them all the time. A mission statement is a constitution that outlines rules of action and a specific purpose or reason for existence. Earlier we discussed the idea that Moses 1:39, "For behold, this is my work and my glory—to bring to pass the immortality and eternal life of man," could be the Lord's mission statement.

Once you've decided through personal study, pondering, and inspiration what your life can and should be, it is much easier to make decisions about how to spend your time and where to put your energies. Comedienne Lily Tomlin once quipped, " I always wanted to be somebody, but I should have been more specific."[10] A mission statement is more specific. It tells you what to say "yes" to, making it a lot easier to say "no" to those things that do not contribute to or may distract you from your objectives. Further, a mission statement can keep you focused on the tree of life and prevent you from getting lost in "strange roads" or "forbidden paths" (1 Nephi 8:28, 32).

When we involve the Lord in our mission statements and make his purposes part of our purpose, our mission becomes a co-mission. Some are hesitant to give their whole lives to the Lord, thinking somehow they may be sacrificing something. The Doctrine and Covenants warns against the latter-day condition in which "every man walketh in his own way" (D&C 1:16). President Benson taught that if we really want to be successful, in the best sense of the word, walking in the Lord's way is the smartest thing we can do:

> Men and women who turn their lives over to God will discover that He can make a lot more out of their lives than they can. He will deepen their joys, expand their vision, quicken their minds, strengthen their muscles, lift their spirits, multiply their blessings, increase their opportunities, comfort their souls, raise up friends, and pour out peace. Whoever will lose his life in the service of God will find eternal life (see Matthew 10:39).[11]

It might be a good idea to write your mission statement in pencil because pondering our path is not a one-time exercise. Because the elements will combine to throw us off course, constant monitoring and course corrections may be necessary. I remember reading that an airliner is off-course *most* of the time, but because of constant course corrections it eventually touches down on the right runway. Similarly, our path pondering should be done constantly to make sure the path we're on is leading us toward the destination we desire.

A few years ago, I remember sharing a home teaching message written by President Thomas S. Monson. He spoke of the legendary World War II German battleship named the *Bismarck* and how quickly it sent opposing ships to the bottom of the sea. However, during a famous battle, a torpedo scored a lucky hit on the ship's rudder, rendering it unable to steer. All the mighty battleship could do was go in circles. Because it wasn't going anywhere, Allied ships pounded it with artillery until it eventually sank.[12]

Without a course or destination, all of our mighty potential may do nothing but go in circles. The Prophet Joseph Smith observed, "You know, brethren, that a very large ship is benefited very much by a very small helm in the time of a storm, by being kept workways with the wind and the waves" (D&C 123:16; James 3:4).

Regardless of the wind and waves, we can reach our destination with help from a very small helm—a course, a purpose, a destination. A helm is part of the steering mechanism, and with our scriptures, our patriarchal blessing, and the Holy Ghost, we can ponder the path of our feet, chart our divine destination and mission, and get under way on a course that will bless our families and build the kingdom.

SCRIPTURE THREE:

"Thou shalt not idle away thy time, neither shalt thou bury thy talent that it may not be known" (D&C 60:13)

It's clear from the scriptures that the Lord is concerned with how we spend our time. Amulek testified, "If we do not improve our time while in this life, then cometh the night of darkness wherein there can be no labor performed" (Alma 34:33).

The key to improving our time lies with adjusting our idle. Most of us need to adjust our idle. When a car is sitting at a stoplight, it's idling. The engine is on and running, but it's not delivering any power. The V6 in my minivan can take my family over Parley's Summit at 65 miles per hour without shifting down. That's a lot of power. But at a stoplight, it just idles. Its tremendous power is at a standstill. Most of us are like that at times.

The Lord's displeasure with idleness is mentioned several times in the scriptures:

> Now, I, the Lord, am not well pleased with the inhabitants of Zion, for there are idlers among them; and their children are also growing up in wickedness; they also seek not earnestly the riches of eternity, but their eyes are full of greediness. (D&C 68:31)

> Let every man be diligent in all things. And the idler shall not have place in the church, except he repent and mend his ways. (D&C 75:29)

> Thou shalt not be idle; for he that is idle shall not eat the bread nor wear the garments of the laborer. (D&C 42:42)

> Behold, this was the iniquity of thy sister Sodom, pride, fulness of bread, and abundance of idleness was in her and in her daughters, neither did she strengthen the hand of the poor and needy. (Ezekiel 16:49)

Elder John Longden once observed, "Satan selects his disciples when they are idle; Jesus selected his when they were busy at their work."[13] A similar thought is expressed in a song by professor Harold Hill in *The Music Man*. While trying to convince the townspeople of the trouble in River City, Professor Hill repeated an old English proverb, "Oh, the idle brain is the devil's playground."

Idleness and the relentless pursuit of leisure time isn't just a lifestyle choice, it's a sin. In fact, it's a tragedy. President Gordon B. Hinckley has taught:

> One of the great tragedies we witness almost daily is the tragedy of men of high aim and low achievement. Their motives are noble. Their proclaimed ambition is praiseworthy. Their capacity is great. But their discipline is weak. They succumb to indolence. Appetite robs them of will.[14]

The latter half of Scripture Three, "nor bury thy talent that it may not be known," is intriguing. It seems to me that the best possible use of our talents would be to help build the kingdom. But you can't build anything if you're always on break. Idleness buries talents. Brother Stephen R. Covey has written:

> Too many vacations that last too long, too many movies, too much TV, too much video game playing—too much undisciplined leisure time in which a person continually takes the

course of least resistance gradually wastes a life. It ensures that a person's capacities stay dormant, that talents remain undeveloped, that the mind and spirit become lethargic and that the heart is unfulfilled.[15]

Brigham Young remarked, "Your time . . . is property that belongs to the Lord . . . and if [you] do not make good use of it [you] shall be held accountable."[16] The average American watches more than four hours of television per day. What would happen if we spent more time developing our talents than watching others develop theirs? We could spend more time strengthening our marriage than watching *The Bachelor*, more time working on our musical gifts than worshiping *American Idol*, and more time developing our skills for spiritual survival than watching *Survivor*. What could be more exciting than discovering and developing a new skill? We could use our abilities to serve others, bless our neighbors, and build the kingdom. Why did the Lord give us talents if not to bless one another with them and use them to proclaim the gospel?

Anyone who carefully reads the Book of Mormon will begin to notice that wickedness and laziness go hand in hand. When the people become indolent, they are called wicked. When they become prideful, they also become lazy. They would rather hunt than farm (farming is a lot more work), and they seek to put others in bondage so they can "glut themselves with the labors of" others (Mosiah 9:12; 2 Nephi 5:24; Alma 17:15; Alma 22:28).

Because wickedness and idleness are synonyms, we may well say that *idleness never was happiness.* Lying around, sitting around, and hanging out never made anyone a happier person, though it has made several rounder. Og Mandino said it beautifully: "Activity and sadness are eternal opposites."[17]

And if it's rest you're looking for, remember that idleness makes us more tired, not less. Sir Arthur Conan Doyle observed, "I never remember feeling tired by work, though idleness exhausts me completely."[18]

Scripture Three reminds us to adjust our idle. Each of us has great potential to climb over summits and fly over steep grades. Sitting and idling at crossroads is a waste of power and a waste of life. As President Kimball once said, "We have paused on some plateaus long enough. Let us resume our journey forward and upward."[19]

SCRIPTURE FOUR:
"This is my work" (Moses 1:39)

The opposite of idleness is industry. Our Heavenly Father has all power, yet he has not chosen to retire. He possesses all things, yet he does not spend eternity in idleness. As we've already discussed, the Lord describes his mission in these words: "This is my *work* and my glory." I suspect that if we are to become like God, we will get there, at least in part, by working.

It seems that for many, the principle of work is declining in popularity. The relentless pursuit of leisure time has become the goal of a new generation. But most people ultimately discover that there is little satisfaction to be found in a labor-free lifestyle. Some have retired after winning the lottery, only to find that they return to work after a month or two out of sheer boredom. Og Mandino has written:

> You were not created for a life of idleness. You cannot eat from sunrise to sunset or drink or play. . . . Work is not your enemy but your friend. If all manners of labor were forbidden to thee you would fall to your knees and beg an early death. . . . You may work grudgingly or you may work gratefully; you may work as a human or you may work as an animal.[20]

We must work to make it through this life, but we alone decide whether to view our work as a blessing or a curse, to work as a human or as an animal. President David O. McKay said, "Let us realize that the privilege to work is a gift, that power to work is a blessing, that love of work is success."[21]

President Gordon B. Hinckley reminded us that the origin of our work in mortality began with the fall of man: "Jehovah established the law when He declared, 'In the sweat of thy face shalt thou eat bread' (Genesis 3:19)." This law has often been called the "gospel of work." President Hinckley continued:

> I believe in the gospel of work. There is no substitute under the heavens for productive labor. It is the process by which dreams become reality. It is the process by which idle visions become dynamic achievements. We are all inherently lazy. We would rather play than work. We would rather loaf than work. A little play and a little loafing are good—that is one of the reasons you are here. But it is work that spells the difference in the life of a man or woman. It is stretching our minds and utilizing the skills of our hands that lifts us from the stagnation of mediocrity.[22]

What kind of work should we do? We discussed that question a few pages ago while talking about Scripture Two, "Ponder the path of thy feet." But the goal isn't only to work hard at something. Some illegal drug dealers probably put in lots of hours. The goal is to work toward worthy objectives.

I remember hearing a story as a child that made quite an impression on me. A scientist conducted an experiment with what are called "processionary caterpillars." Processionary caterpillars follow one another in a kind of follow-the-leader fashion as they look for food. The scientist somehow succeeded in arranging these creatures around the rim of a flowerpot. They followed each other in circles for several days until they eventually died of starvation. Food was only inches away, in the center of the flowerpot, but they all died while appearing very busy. I remember well the lesson: *They died because they confused activity with accomplishment.* Again, the goal isn't just to be busy, but to be busy doing something worthwhile.

Once you find a purpose in life, a marvelous work in which to engage, your work becomes a mission and a pleasure. Perhaps your passion is to become a successful wife and mother and raise a family, or to become a world-class husband and father (that's my goal). We all know the oft-repeated statement that the most important work we will ever do "will be within the walls of [our] own home."[23] The world might not view gospel goals as particularly glamorous, but we recognize them as part of the work and glory of God. Once we know what we want to do, we go at it with everything we've got. George Bernard Shaw observed that true joy does not come from pursuing pleasure but from working toward what you have chosen as your life's mission:

> This is the true joy in life, the being used for a purpose recognized by yourself as a mighty one; the being thoroughly worn out before you are thrown on the scrap heap; the being a force of Nature instead of a feverish, selfish little clod of ailments and grievances complaining that the world will not devote itself to making you happy.[24]

Perhaps the greatest reward of work is satisfaction. It's always been interesting to me that after the Lord created the world, he said, "And I, God, saw everything that I had made, and, behold, all things which I had made were very good" (Moses 2:31). Even the Lord took a moment to look over his work. On a scale a little less grand, what gives greater satisfaction than looking over a freshly mowed and trimmed lawn, or a remodeled room, or the performance of a son or daughter after being inspired (and perhaps pushed) by their parents to practice?

Margaret Thatcher observed, "Look at a day when you are supremely satisfied at the end. It's not a day when you lounge around doing nothing; it's when you've had everything to do, and you've done it."[25] Robert Louis

Stevenson agreed: "I know what pleasure is, for I have done good work."[26]

Someone once remarked that if you see a man on top of a mountain, you know he didn't fall there. Rewards don't come in an instant, and neither does satisfaction unless effort is expended. Longfellow wrote, "The heights by great men reached and kept were not attained by sudden flight, but they, while their companions slept, were toiling upward in the night."[27]

Longfellow's statement reminds us of how Helaman and his two thousand stripling warriors successfully retook the city of Manti because they "toiled upward in the night" and marched "while their companions" (in this case, their enemies) slept (Alma 58:26–28).[28]

Sometimes work is hard, tedious, and even painful. In those situations the only thing that can keep us going is anticipating the satisfaction of a job well done. Some individuals work for many years to accomplish a singular goal. Olympic athletes prepare for a lifetime for their one moment. I don't consider myself a fan of boxing, but I appreciate the idea expressed by Muhammad Ali: "I hated every minute of the training, but I said, 'Don't quit. Suffer now and live the rest of your life as a champion.'"[29]

The philosopher Korsaren believed that work was the antidote for just about any malady in life:

If you are poor, work. If you are burdened with seemingly unfair responsibilities, work. If you are happy, work. Idleness gives room for doubts and fears. If disappointments come, keep right on working. If sorrow overwhelms you and loved ones seem not true, work. If health is threatened, work. When faith falters and reason fails, just work. When dreams are shattered and hope seems dead, work. Work as if your life were in peril. It really is. No matter what ails you, work. Work faithfully—work with faith. Work is the greatest remedy available for both mental and physical afflictions.[30]

I honor anyone who works. I see young people flipping burgers or mowing lawns, and I honor them for working. There are so many less honorable things they could be doing. If I have one fear concerning the youth of the Church, it is that they are not learning to work and therefore not finding joy and satisfaction in their work. Many young men are masters at video and computer games, they can navigate the Internet like Magellan, and they know how to play and be entertained all day long. When these same young men begin their missions, they are suddenly expected to put in more than twelve hours a day in difficult and often monotonous work. Many of them experience depression because of their inability to perform at a level they've never attempted or experienced before.

I used to tease my parents about what they asked me to do the day before I entered the Missionary Training Center. I must have hauled a dozen wheelbarrows full of cow manure up our sloping front lawn to the gardens in the back. When I finally put my calloused hands and aching back to bed that night, I said to myself, "I can't wait to go on a mission where I can get a break!"

I don't tease my parents anymore. In fact, I thank my Heavenly Father for a mother and father who loved me enough to put me to work. I could labor as hard as the proverbial farm boy from Idaho, even though I was just a city boy from Salt Lake. That work ethic especially blessed me the day the 747 lifted off the runway at Manila International Airport to bring me home. I reclined my seat and closed my eyes with the peaceful assurance that I had worked hard on my mission. I knew it, and I knew that God knew it. That was a comforting feeling of satisfaction I will never forget.

Scripture Four reminds us that work is honorable and good and that God is still working on our behalf. Work is an important part of the gospel of Jesus Christ. We have no hymn that says, "Relaxation is great" or "Hanging around is blessed," but we do have one titled "Sweet is the

Work."[31] Our work as parents in behalf of our families, our Church, and our brothers and sisters is perhaps the sweetest work of all.

SCRIPTURE FIVE:
"I will go and do" (1 Nephi 3:7)

There is a time to ponder, and there is a time to produce. After Nephi received his marching orders, he went right to work. His assignment was not easy: He had to hike approximately two hundred miles in a desert and get the plates of brass from a man who would probably try to kill him. Nephi's response to the Lord's request? "I will go and do."

Among the many admirable traits Nephi possessed, one of my favorites is his initiative. Once the Lord gave him a commandment, Nephi went into action, and he continued to act even when unexpected problems hedged the way. He did not obtain the brass plates easily, but he persisted until he did.

When Nephi broke his bow, instead of sitting around murmuring like the rest of the family, he "did make out of wood a bow, and out of a straight stick, an arrow" (1 Nephi 16:23). If you look closely at that verse, you'll notice that footnote "a" refers you to the Topical Guide and the word "Initiative."

Nephi could have given up after he broke his bow,

complaining to the Lord, "Now what do I do?" But he didn't. He remembered the commandment and relied on his faith that God would prepare a way. In his own words, Nephi was "led by the Spirit, not knowing beforehand the things which [he] should do" (1 Nephi 4:6). He preferred making tracks rather than making excuses. He took the initiative and moved ahead.

President Marion G. Romney observed, "While the Lord will magnify us in both subtle and dramatic ways, he can only guide our footsteps when we move our feet."[32] Some of us want results without work. That's backward. As Robert Anthony once observed, you can't stand in front of your fireplace and demand, "Give me heat, then I'll give you wood."[33]

Many of us want to wait for a revelation before we go anywhere, but perhaps revelation requires a little action first. Elder John H. Groberg taught a wonderful principle, the application of which is largely responsible for the fact that there's a wedding ring on my left hand:

> In the past I have tried to figure out whether I should go into business or into teaching or into the arts or whatever. As I have begun to proceed along one path, having more or less gathered what facts I could, I have found that if that decision was wrong or was

146

taking me down the wrong path—not necessarily an evil one, but one that was not right for me—without fail, the Lord has always let me know just this emphatically: "That is wrong; do not go that way. That is not for you!"

On the other hand, there may have been two or three ways that I could have gone, any one of which would have been right and would have been in the general area providing the experience and means whereby I could fulfill the mission that the Lord had in mind for me. Because he knows we need the growth, he generally does not point and say, "Open that door and go twelve yards in that direction; then turn right and go two miles . . ." But if it is wrong, he will let us know—we will feel it for sure. I am positive of that. So rather than saying, "I will not move until I have this burning in my heart," let us turn it around and say, "I will move unless I feel it is wrong; and if it is wrong, then I will not do it." By eliminating all of these wrong courses, very quickly you will find yourself going in the direction that you ought to be going, and then you can receive the assurance: "Yes, I am going in the right direction. I am doing what my Father in Heaven wants me to do because I am not doing the things he does not want me to do." And you can know that for sure. That is part of the growth process and part of accomplishing what our Father in Heaven has in mind for us.[34]

Sometimes you have to get going before you get guidance. I've always loved the story of the healing of the ten lepers recorded in Luke. When they asked the Savior for mercy, he told them to "go" and "shew [themselves] unto the priests" (Luke 17:14). Jesus' instructions are interesting because visiting the priests is what the lepers would be required to do *after* they were healed in order to be readmitted to society.[35] But Jesus asked them to find the priests *before* they were healed.

The lepers might have responded, "We can't show ourselves to the priests; we're not healed yet!" Instead, they decided to "go and do" what Jesus suggested. Luke records, "And it came to pass, that, *as they went*, they were cleansed" (Luke 17:14; emphasis added). The scripture doesn't say, "And it came to pass, that as they just stood there, they were cleansed." It says, "As they *went*, they were cleansed." As someone once said, "God cannot steer a parked car." There's something magical about moving forward with faith. W. H. Murray wrote:

> Until one is committed there is hesitancy, the chance to draw back, always ineffectiveness. Concerning all acts of initiative (and creation), there is one elementary truth, the ignorance of which kills countless ideas and splendid plans: that the moment one definitely commits oneself, then Providence moves too. All sorts of things occur to help one that would never otherwise have occurred. A whole stream of events issue from the decision, raising in one's favor all manner of unforeseen incidents and material assistance, which no man could have dreamt would have come his way.[36]

All of this talk of going and doing can become a little tiring. Some of us feel that all of our "get up and go" got up and went years ago. But fatigue doesn't result from doing things—it results from not doing things, or more specifically, from not finishing things.

> Do you want to know where fatigue comes from? It doesn't come from working too hard. All the research shows that fatigue comes from

not finishing your work. William James once wrote, "Nothing is so fatiguing as the eternal hanging on of an uncompleted task."[37]

Indeed, to "go and do" is much less exhausting than to "sit and stew." Watch for the word *go* in the following verses: The Lord encouraged Moses, "Therefore *go*, and I will be with thy mouth, and teach thee what thou shalt say" (Exodus 4:12). When Enoch complained that he was slow of speech, the Lord said, "*Go* forth and do as I have commanded thee" (Moses 6:32). Isaiah admonished the house of Israel, "*Go* ye forth of Babylon" (Isaiah 48:20). Lehi told Nephi, "Therefore *go*, my son, and thou shalt be favored" (1 Nephi 3:6). Jesus told the centurion, "*Go* thy way; and as thou hast believed, so be it done unto thee" (Matthew 8:13). The parable of the good Samaritan concluded when Jesus told the lawyer, "*Go*, and do thou likewise" (Luke 10:37). The resurrected Christ told the apostles, "*Go* ye therefore, and teach all nations" (Matthew 28:19).

These scriptures encourage not only action but also direction. When Jesus asked the twelve, "Will ye also go away?" Peter answered, "Lord, to whom shall we go? thou hast the words of eternal life" (John 6:67–68).

Dr. Brent Barlow once suggested that we could attach another meaning to the acronym LDS: "Let's Do

Something!"[38] Indeed, let's go and do! "Gospel inaction" is an oxymoron, and "gospel in action" is redundant. We live in a world where there is always something righteous we can go and do. There are people to be loved, children to be raised, families to be taught, hearts to be lifted, and knees to be strengthened. Going and doing will keep us active and positive. Elder Marion D. Hanks taught that the best antidote for feeling down is to get up and go:

> At the moment of depression, if you will follow a simple program, you will get out of it. Get on your knees and get the help of God; then get up and go find somebody who needs something that you can help them find. Then it will be a good day.[39]

I remember as a young man being told that President Spencer W. Kimball had this two-word motto on his desk: "Do it." Those two words have become quite well known as the slogan of an athletic shoe company. But I think I like the phrase best as it appears in an Old Testament verse that provides the perfect ending for this discussion on Scripture Five: "Arise; for this matter belongeth unto thee: we also will be with thee: be of good courage, and do it" (Ezra 10:4).

CONCLUSION

I love the old adage, "Some people dream of doing great things. Others wake up and do them." I've read a number of motivational books and listened to a few motivational seminars while traveling in my car, but nothing gets me going like the scriptures. As Latter-day Saints, we are involved in the greatest work in the universe, and time is running out. Who can sleep through the last days when words such as "Awake and arise from the dust" thunder from the last page of the Book of Mormon? (Moroni 10:31). Aroused from a spiritual slumber, we "ponder the path of our feet" (Proverbs 4:26), fully aware of the commandment, "Thou shalt not idle away thy time" (D&C 60:13). Then we're off to work, knowing the "work and glory" of God is to help all of his children reach their highest potential (Moses 1:39). Finally, we "go and do" (1 Nephi 3:7) with a happy heart, anticipating that one day we will hear the words, "Well done, thou good and faithful servant" (Matthew 25:21).

This little book contains twenty-five of my favorite scriptures and most of my favorite quotations. And yet, I feel I have barely scratched the surface. I suspect that any member of the Church could find twenty-five different scriptures for each of these same topics. Because of the breadth and depth of the standard works, I am thrilled, encouraged, and intimidated all at the same time. There is so much to learn.

It's difficult to imagine how we could build a happy, healthy philosophy of life without the scriptures and the words of the prophets. They teach the plan of happiness, they bless our families and our marriages, and they help us endure when times are tough. Most important, they help us strengthen our testimonies of Jesus Christ, the central figure in the plan of salvation and our only hope for happiness here and hereafter. As we learn of him and listen to his words, we find meaning and motivation in our lives, and we are blessed with the faith and power not only to survive but also to thrive and rejoice.

NOTES

1. Brigham Young, in *Journal of Discourses*, 26 vols. (London: Latter-day Saints' Book Depot, 1854–86), 12:104.

2. Heber C. Kimball, in *Journal of Discourses*, 10:167–68.

3. Sterling W. Sill, *The Majesty of Books* (Salt Lake City: Deseret Book, 1974), 147.

4. In *Quotationary* (Midway, Utah: Novasoft, 1999), CD-ROM; emphasis added.

5. Bruce R. McConkie, *The Millennial Messiah: The Second Coming of the Son of Man* (Salt Lake City: Deseret Book, 1982), 31.

6. *Children's Songbook* (Salt Lake City: The Church of Jesus Christ of Latter-day Saints, 1989), no. 196.

7. Alonzo L. Gaskill, *The Lost Language of Symbolism* (Salt Lake City: Deseret Book, 2003), 37.

8. Ezra Taft Benson, "To the Young Women of the Church," *Ensign*, November 1986, 82.

9. Elaine L. Jack, "Identity of a Young Woman," *Ensign*, November 1989, 87; emphasis added.

10. In John Roger and Peter McWilliams, *Do It! Let's Get Off Our Butts* (Los Angeles: Prelude Press, 1991), 256.

11. Ezra Taft Benson, *The Teachings of Ezra Taft Benson* (Salt Lake City: Bookcraft, 1988), 361.

12. Thomas S. Monson, "Sailing Safely on the Seas of Life," *Ensign*, July 1999, 2–5.

13. John Longden, in Conference Reports of The Church of Jesus Christ of Latter-day Saints (Salt Lake City: The Church of Jesus Christ of Latter-day Saints, 1898 to present), April 1966, 39.

14. Gordon B. Hinckley, *Be Thou an Example* (Salt Lake City: Deseret Book, 1981), 60.

15. Stephen R. Covey, *The Seven Habits of Highly Effective People* (New York: Simon & Schuster, 1989), 115.

16. Brigham Young, *Discourses of Brigham Young*, sel. John A. Widtsoe (Salt Lake City: Deseret Book, 1954), 254.

17. Og Mandino, *The Greatest Success in the World* (New York: Bantam Books, 1981), 76.

18. *The Forbes Book of Business Quotations* (New York: Black Dog & Leventhal Publishers, 1997), 437.

19. Spencer W. Kimball, "Let Us Move Forward and Upward," *Ensign*, May 1979, 82.

20. Og Mandino, *The Greatest Success in the World*, 66.

21. David O. McKay, *Pathways to Happiness* (Salt Lake City: Bookcraft, 1957), 381.

22. Gordon B. Hinckley, *Teachings of Gordon B. Hinckley* (Salt Lake City: Deseret Book, 1997), 704–5.

23. Harold B. Lee, "Follow the Leadership of the Church," *Ensign*, July 1973, 98.

24. George Bernard Shaw, in William I. Nichols, *Words to Live By* (New York: Simon and Schuster, 1949) 79.

25. This quote is widely attributed to Margaret Thatcher, but the author has been unable to find an original source for it.

26. In Sterling W. Sill, *The Laws of Success* (Salt Lake City: Deseret Book, 1975), 62.

27. Henry Wadsworth Longfellow, "The Ladder of St. Augustine," in *Longfellow: Poems and Other Writings* (New York: The Library of America, 2000), 325–26.

28. For further discussion on this topic, see John Bytheway, *Righteous Warriors* (Salt Lake City: Deseret Book, 2004), 126–29.

29. In Cynthia Kersey, *Unstoppable* (Naperville, Ill.: Sourcebooks, 1998), 158.

30. *The Forbes Book of Business Quotations*, 928.

31. *Hymns of The Church of Jesus Christ of Latter-day Saints* (Salt Lake City: The Church of Jesus Christ of Latter-day Saints, 1985), no. 147.

32. Marion G. Romney, "The Basic Principles of Church Welfare," *Ensign*, May 1981, 91.

33. Robert Anthony, *Doing What You Love, Loving What You Do* (Random House Audio Publishing, 1991), audiocassette, side one.

34. John H. Groberg, "What Is Your Mission?" *1979 Devotional Speeches of the Year* (Provo, Utah: Brigham Young University Press, 1980), 97–98.

35. James E. Talmage, *Jesus the Christ* (Salt Lake City: Deseret Book, 1976), 471.

36. W. H. Murray, in Neal A. Maxwell, *That My Family Should Partake* (Salt Lake City: Deseret Book, 1974), 27.

37. Steve Chandler, *100 Ways to Motivate Yourself* (St. Paul, Minn.: HighBridge, 1996), audiocassette.

38. Brent Barlow, *Worth Waiting For: Sexual Abstinence before Marriage* (Salt Lake City: Deseret Book, 1995), 9.

39. Marion D. Hanks, "Make It a Good Day!" *BYU Speeches of the Year, 1966–1967* (Provo, Utah: Brigham Young University Press, 1967), 7.

INDEX